Procession of the Virgin.

THE STORY

OF THE

FAITH IN HUNGARY.

BY THE AUTHOR OF
"FROM DAWN TO DARK IN ITALY."

PHILADELPHIA:
PRESBYTERIAN BOARD OF PUBLICATION,
No. 821 CHESTNUT STREET.

WESTCOTT &
THOMSON
STEREOTYPERS
PHILADA

CONTENTS.

CHAPTER XX.

CHAPTER XXI.

CHAPTER XXII.

CHAPTER XXIII.

CHAPTER XXIV.

CHAPTER XXV.

CHAPTER XXVI.

CHAPTER XXVII.

CHAPTER XXVIII.

CHAPTER XXIX.

CHAPTER XXX.

CHAPTER XXXI.

CHAPTER XXXII.

CHAPTER XXXIII.

CHAPTER XXXIV.

CHAPTER XXXV.

CHAPTER XXXVI.

CHAPTER XXXVII.

CHAPTER XXXVIII.

CHAPTER XXXIX.

PREFACE.

"A BRANCH of the great family of the gospel has been forgotten by the rest," writes Merle d'Aubignè of the Hungarian Reformed Church. The accusation is true. Who knows anything of her creeds and her martyrs—of her struggles for the truth, her trials and her triumphs? She has dropped completely out of the reckoning of her sister churches, yet not one of them all (except perhaps the Vaudois) made a longer or a braver fight for the faith once delivered to the saints.

Few English Christians are aware how very nearly a Protestant land Hungary had once become. Only three families among all her magnates were Roman Catholics, and the proportion of Reformed among her people was thirty to one when our Queen Elizabeth ascended the English throne. But priest and potentate used all the arts of evil to suppress the religion of the Bible with too much success, for a time.

"The Story of the Faith in Hungary" was written before the startling events of the last war. Since the defeat and humiliation of Austria, the position of Hungary is no longer that of an oppressed province of the empire, at the mercy of the Jesuits who influenced the counsels of its rulers at Vienna. The coronation of the emperor at

Pesth as king of Hungary is an acknowledgment of the ancient rights and privileges of the Magyar people. Let us hope that the political changes of the last few years will secure the religious as well as the civil liberties of the Hungarians, and that Protestant and evangelical truth will flourish throughout the land.

But let us begin the chequered story.

THE FAITH IN HUNGARY.

CHAPTER I.

HEATHEN HUNGARY.

THE Romans called it Dacia when their emperor Trajan conquered it and sent colonies thither. Remnants of his bridges, aqueducts and military roads yet remain, dating from a hundred years after the Christian era.

Those colonies were not long-lived, for the blue-eyed Goths swept them away about A.D. 270, and were in their turn overrun by the irresistible Tartar Huns, when every nascent civilization disappeared. Yet even among them did certain pious missionaries in monks' cowls travel from the outlying southern Christianity, and tell them whatever good thing they knew of the religion of our Lord Jesus; but their teaching was so overlaid with ceremony and superstition that it produced little real effect. Another Asiatic tribe of nomad conquerors, the Magyars, came crowding from the teeming East, claiming their descent from the Huns, and in virtue of their strong right hands seizing every town and fastness. The language of these Tartars is that of Hungary at this day—a tongue so widely different from our inflectionized English, and from the German that hems it in and runs over the upper strata of Hungarian society, that the width of the globe might suitably separate between the speakers of each—a living link of relationship with races so remote as even the Mongols that subdued China.

The names of two Christian teachers have come down to us from the chaotic darkness of that age (when deeds of arms were the sole material for fame) as men whose labours were blessed of God. These were Cyril of Illyria and his brother Methodius. They found the Magyars worshipping a fierce war-god as their chief deity, whose symbol was a sword—likewise worshipping the sun and moon, likewise fire. And whereas a family resemblance runs through the heathenish of all lands, these idolaters were used to offer sacrifice on heaped stones, as did the Druids, and amid groves of trees, like the Canaanites and early Greeks; also at lakes and springs of water.

They had soothsayers and augurs. Very slowly spread the truth among them; its precepts of peace and lowliness were most distasteful to the haughty Magyars. It was not as with the nation of Moravia, which espoused the forms of Christianity because their king, Swatopluck, did so at Cyril's teaching. The Magyar spirit had to be broken by successive reverses before it would submit to the new faith. Henry the bird-catcher (a German emperor) slew thirty thousand of them at Merseberg; Otho broke their forces at Augsburg. In the national humbling they forsook their idols numerously. We find in the royal family of this date (950) some Christian names, proving that baptism had penetrated into high places.

Women and captives were God's weak agencies (as elsewhere) for spreading his gospel. Charlotte, daughter of a Christianized Transylvanian prince, was married to the Hungarian regent Geyza, and used all her influence for the cause, until in 977 she had the pleasure of seeing her husband solemnly baptized. Meanwhile, scattered among his subjects were scores of prisoners from the German wars—some of them priests, who published on all sides their religion. Thus quietly was a reforming work being done, until Geyza, with rash zeal, orders a national baptism in the Moravian style above mentioned. His subjects rebel, and the well-meaning king has strife for all his days—strife which is transmitted with the crown to his son Stephen, afterward surnamed the Saint; the pious son of a pious mother, which is a connection frequent enough to seem like a naming of effect and cause. Even now, after a lapse of eight centuries and a half, he is the blessed hero of Hungarian hearts. No king will they acknowledge whose brow is not circled with St. Stephen's crown, and on the day of his coronation he must ascend the tumulus outside Presburg with the sword of St. Stephen in his hand, wherewith to cut a cross in the air, while he repeats St. Stephen's vow, and on the fête-day of the latter (20th August) that national Hungarian relic, his *hand*, is paraded solemnly through Buda and Pesth, in a procession with much pomp of priesthood and state officials.

What did Stephen to earn this protracted remembrance? More than most monarchs on whom fame attends: he encouraged the spread of the Christian religion in his land by every means in his power; he divided his realm into counties and circuits, over which he placed palatines and judges; he established schools and secured the rights of property. These were vast boons in that wild age, when as yet Dane and Saxon disputed the English sceptre. But Charlemagne had set a bad example of the royal method of conversion by force, and lesser princes were apt to imitate him. Stephen of Hungary issued an edict commanding his people to change their religion under heavy penalties. This to the free and independent Magyars, with the wild blood of the desert coursing among them still! These dwellers of the "heaths" and forest villages (pagani) were yet "heathen" and pagan in the deepest sense. Still they had traditions of that hurricane-rush along the north shores of the Euxine into Pannonia, and of Arpad their leader, and the sun-worship of the horde: they rose en masse against Stephen and his edict.

The ruins of a Benedictine monastery yet stand which he built and endowed in acknowledgment of his victory over them. Thenceforward throughout Hungary the Sabbath-day was observed, so that all cattle and implements found doing work were confiscated. Pope Sylvester sent him the aforesaid crown, calling it "holy and apostolic," and congratulating him on the establishment of Christianity.

But for fifty years thereafter the struggle with

paganism went on. Andrew the First was invited to fill the throne, on condition that he would overthrow Christianity.

There is a huge rock at Buda, rising jagged from the Danube's edge over that fine city, and named by Germans the Blocksberg: an observatory now stands on its summit. But on the same site, long ago, a holy hermit established himself, and went about the neighbouring district teaching his religion; and during these wars in Andrew's time he was flung from the brow of the Blocksberg into the broad current beneath, by some of the savage Magyars whom he sought to convert. Whence the peak is still called St. Gellert's Hill.

King Ladislaus, in 1080, was yet contending with heathen Hungarians. Such choice as Mohammed offered in his conquests—"the Koran or the sword"—was also the offer of Ladislaus to those whom he subdued—"baptism or death." The former alternative was largely preferred, and the king was canonized for his wholesale conversions.

It was a good thing to supplant paganism by any species of Christianity, so far as this world's gear is concerned. The old sacrifices at stones and streams, and to the war-god, became extinct before the year 1100.

CHAPTER II.

THE WALDENSES IN HUNGARY.

AS God has never left himself without witness during even the darkest times, so while the Christian Church was slowly corrupting into the Greek and Romish apostasies, a band of believers called Paulicians had appeared to uphold the purity of the gospel. From Asia Minor they penetrated into Thrace, Bulgaria, Croatia—lineal ancestors to the Albigenses, among whom Peter Waldo was the most renowned teacher. According to the testimony of those enemies who burned and crucified them in hundreds, they denied the orthodox faith, inasmuch as they would not adore the mother of God nor believe the sacramental bread to be Christ's body. We find these heretics abundant in Hungary about 1176; and their numbers were recruited by refugees from France and Italy, trying to escape the sword of Pope Innocent III. Dalmatia and Bosnia were full of these unfortunates, who appealed for protection to the ban, and to his superior lord, Emerich, king of Hungary.

The pope sent a bloodthirsty demand for them, couched (according to his wont) in sweet language. But the ban's own wife had joined them, the bishop of Bosnia had joined them, ten thousand Dalmatians had joined them—how was it possible to obey? Then the king of Hungary was ordered to let loose his soldiers upon the heretics, and there wanted but the sinful subservience of one man to repeat such vast crimes as Simon de Montfort and the monk Dominic perpetrated in Languedoc. Emerich refused to shed innocent blood, and Bosnia was for some time a safe refuge for the Waldenses, who travelled about in the neighbouring states with their "good news," and made so many converts among the peasantry and lesser nobles that the Hungarian hierarchy at last called out for the Inquisition.

Tides of crusaders passed through the country at intervals during these years. One Hungarian king joined them with some thousands of Magyar cavalry; he brought home a quantity of the most approved relics, and the daughter of the Greek emperor to be the wife of his son and successor, Bela.

CHAPTER III.

THE GOLDEN BULL.

JUST what Magna Charta is in English history, the "Golden Bull" is in Hungarian. The inferior nobles rose against the tyranny of this crusading king (who, like our John, while a slave to the pope, was a despot to his subjects), and forced him to grant them sundry privileges, or rather to confirm their liberties. It was only seven years after Runnymede that this similar transaction between prince and people took place in distant Hungary, and on it are based all the rights of the nobles, or freemen, at the present hour.

The priesthood acquired by it freedom from taxation, and tithes of corn and wine payable in kind for ever; and the last article of the charter recognized the right of the nation to resist in case the king should fail in his oath to observe it. Speedily the nobles had occasion to put in practice this provision; for the crusading king (carrying out his resemblance to John Lackland) seized every opportunity of infringement. He gave the farming of the revenues to Mohammedans and pagans, who, copying their Christian neighbours, oppressed the people to make them change their religion. The pope exhorted the king about this and much other misconduct, and at last the archbishop of Grán laid the country under interdict.

All squabbles were stopped by a crushing calamity. Half a million of wild Mongols crossed the Carpathians and like a flood surged over Hungary. They came flushed with conquest from Moscow and Moravia. A tremendous defeat was suffered by the Magyar army, and for a year the Tartars had the kingdom at their mercy. Devastation was their delight. "Some of the inhabitants fled to the marshes and impenetrable forests; the rest were butchered without exception. When the remnant began to return from their hiding-places, they found the wild beasts so numerous that wolves took infants out of the cradle! The plague broke out, and swarms of locusts came devouring every green thing; the people lived on carrion—nay, even human flesh was publicly sold in the market! A terrible judgment of God lay on the land."

Yet when it was thus miserably exhausted after the retreat of the Tartars, did Pope Gregory IX. command the Hungarian king to go on crusade against the heretic king of Bulgaria. Bela declined: his hands were quite full enough of home-work, and to get his people bread and houses seemed to him more important than killing Waldenses.

At Ofen (which is Buda, but so called from the hot springs) these heretics had become so numerous, that upon the papal legate's publishing a severe edict against them, he found it prudent to leave the city. The Inquisition had been introduced, but failed to work well while so much popular power remained. Each noble, by the Golden Bull, was protected from all arbitrary imprisonment, and only the king had power of life and death. These circumstances deprived the Inquisition of its most terrible prerogatives, and reduced it to a mere court of inquiry; which, indeed, is the pretence of its name.

A Hungarian martyr, named Simeon Scaliger, was at this period burned in Vienna (just beyond the frontier) for teaching the truth. It was as if to show what the ecclesiastics would do within the frontier if they dared.

CHAPTER IV.

HUSSITES IN HUNGARY.

THE freedom of the Hungarian constitution, warranted by the Golden Bull, caused the country to become a nest of refugees. The persecuted Hussites of Bohemia fled thither, and wherever they settled, fresh heretics sprang up with doctrines intolerable to the clergy. No purgatory, no prayers for the dead, no images, no confessional, no worship of saints, no pope—these men anticipated all the reforms of the Reformation. They were compelled to defend themselves in Bohemia, and defeated the imperial troops eleven times successively under Ziska, but finally he led the remnants of his army into the heart of Hungary, and they formed whole colonies, with churches and congregations of their own, under the shadow of the Golden Bull.

Rome could not but be disquieted at their quiet. She stirred up the famous and learned king Matthias Corvinus against them, who not only oppressed these his harmless subjects at her bidding, but also plunged into a war with his father-in-law, Podiebrad of Bohemia, the protector of the Hussites. Yet he refused point-blank to give the pope any rights within his realm other than those already enjoyed; that right of bestowing bishoprics and abbacies, which was staunchly retained by English kings, was likewise firmly grasped by Matthias. And he took delight in such satires on the dominant Church as were written by the bishop of Wardein, surnamed Pannonicus, who sneered at pilgrimage thus:

"O Spaniards, Gauls, Slavonians, Germans, Huns,
Ye seek the gates of him who bears the keys;
Why run so far, ye fools? To enrich the Latin gods?
Is no one saved, then, who remains at home?"

Corvinus founded a library at Ofen, and established a printing-press. For the latter its noblest work might soon have been found in publication of the sacred Scriptures. The Hungarian version lay ready for type. An obscure monk, named Ladislaus Báthory, had some time previously left his brethren of the monastery of St. Paul and retired to a small cavern in the mountain near by; here he lived upon roots, wild fruits and the water of a spring gushing over the rock, while he devoted himself to the translation of the Bible from Latin into Hungarian. No person would he see or speak to, lest it might delay his great performance, whereat tradition declares that he was occupied for the greater part of twenty silent years.

Portions of a translation are also stored in the Imperial Library of Vienna, which were made by two Franciscan monks who fled to Moldavia for shelter because they were Hussites. Christians in those dreary ages instinctively felt that the great cure for the evils of the Church was the diffusion of God's word, which "giveth light and understanding to the simple." Many a monk in the scriptorium of his convent, weary of illuminating missals, and having learning enough for the attempt, tried his hand on rendering into the vulgar tongue of his country the life-giving gospels which comforted himself. And until that word was widely diffused in Hungary there could be nothing but partial illumination; here a few, and there a few, who were happy believers in Christ.

The mass of the nation lodged in such darkness that one hundred and forty holy places possessed images of the Virgin which worked miracles, and which sometimes were carried about from village to village for greater profit. "Superstition was so universal that escape from danger, victory gained, any signal favour whatever was not ascribed to God or Christ, but to Mary, or Martin, or George, or Ladislaus. Some set up public monuments to the saints for their imaginary help, as Prince Báthory in 1489. The numbers of monks who seemed born for nothing else than to eat, were, with their begging habits, a terrible plague to the oppressed country-people, and by their ignorance, superstition and immorality tended to degrade the nation."

Such were the men who dared to persecute the God-fearing Hussites. But in the beginning of the sixteenth century there was a pause—a terrible danger loomed imminent. The Turk had gathered his armies and the shadow of the Crescent fell over the land.

CHAPTER V.

THE CRESCENT AND THE CROSS.

HUNGARY had been the border-land between Paganism and Christianity for many a hundred years: now it was to be the battle-field between the Crescent and the Cross.

A name very well known to Englishmen within the last ten years is that of Varna, which emerged from obscurity with the Crimean War. Once before was it distinguished by the lurid light of battle, when the Turks under Amurad II. conquered the Hungarians under the king Vladislaus. He had shortly before concluded a treaty with the court of Rome, in which he promised that the Hussites in his kingdom should be utterly destroyed, and then, stimulated by the legate-cardinal Julian, under pretext that faith is not to be kept with infidels, he broke his solemnly-sworn truce with the Turks. The latter crime wrought out punishment for the former.

And when the sultan, sitting on horseback in the midst of his janissaries, saw the Hungarian monarch marching down the height to battle, he raised his hands to heaven: "God of the Christians! punish the traitor who dishonoureth thy holy name by breaking his oath!" Vladislaus fell that day, and with him the persecuting legate.

The Hussites had peace for a while amid these storms of warfare. The battle of Belgrade was a victory to the Hungarian king Hunyadi over two hundred thousand Moslems. But the numbers and perseverance of the latter rendered them practically unconquerable; they returned again and again, as the Tartar hordes had done and as locusts march onward despite fire and steel. To this day remain in border counties the fortified churches, whither an alarm-bell summoned the peasants and their families when the first gleam of the dreaded turban and horsetail standard was seen coming through the passes of the Carpathians. A perpetual watchman stood on the little church-tower and the man driving the plough wore a cutlass; and his next act after the sound of the alarm was to gather his cattle as well as his household within the churchyard wall, which was built with battlements and port-holes, frequently with towers. The Moslem cavalry found these humble fortifications often impregnable, because of the breastwork of daring and determined hearts within.

The archbishop of Grán went to Rome, hoping to persuade Leo X. to give help against the Turks. Just then the great treasury of indulgences had been discovered, and the pope made a munificent present of what cost him nothing. Armed with an immense mass of indulgences, the prelate returned to Hungary. Who would go to battle with the infidel?—the commonest soldier might earn unlimited forgiveness of sins by enlisting. And such is the craving of men for the pardon which they know their souls need that a hundred thousand were easily brought together. Without pay, without commissariat, they soon became more dangerous to friends than foes. Their white flag embroidered with the red cross became the standard of a servile war, in which four hundred of the nobility and fourteen bishops perished, with seventy thousand of the peasantry. So the Turks did not receive much harm from this attempt to revive the Crusades, and the least part of the barbarous punishment inflicted on Dorsa, the popular leader, was his being seated on a red-hot throne and crowned with a red-hot crown.

Troops came from Germany to assist the Cross against the Crescent. Among them were many thinking men, who had learned of Luther's ninety-five theses and read his minor works and imbibed the spirit of the Reformation. They sang his hymns as war-songs; they despised the clergy and ridiculed miraculous images. The leaven of the new doctrines spread rapidly, and coalesced with the deep-buried Hussite predilections of the people.

CHAPTER VI.

RISE OF THE REFORMATION.

"THERE was perhaps scarcely any other land," writes the historian, "in which so many persons in so short a time openly forsook the old Church. The Reformation appears at once before us like a powerful stream, and when we search carefully after its source we find it losing itself amid wars and misery—like those rivers of Africa whose springs lie hidden in shifting sands."

The political constitution of Hungary, guaranteed by the Golden Bull, was so framed in the interests of freedom as to render persecution a difficult matter. Presently, Luther's writings were read everywhere, and the priests could do nothing but condemn them from the pulpit; and this very condemnation acted favourably for their spread, because the priests were detested and despised by the nobility, which class comprises all the freeholders of Hungary. There was a wonderful movement in the land. Simon Grynäus, professor in the Royal College at Ofen (which is also Buda), preached publicly "the doctrines which Luther had discovered," as a tolerant Turkish pasha afterward called them. His bishop flung him into prison, but was obliged immediately to set him free again.

"The living word, coming from hearts warmed by conviction, produced a marvellous effect. In a short time whole parishes, villages, towns—yea, perhaps the half of Hungary—declared for the Reformation." In one parish the preaching of a German pastor induced the entire mining population to become Lutherans, and they at once established communion in both kinds. Count Mark Pempflinger had a quarrel with the archbishop of Grán, and to spite him encouraged the new teachers in his towns and protected the readers of Luther's books. "Notwithstanding, every way, whether in pretence or in truth, Christ was preached," and "much people was added unto the Lord."

Two Silesian monks, who had been to Wittemberg and learned from Luther's self, travelled about the country with the word of God in their hands, and converted the head-knowledge of many a citizen and peasant noble into the heart-knowledge of true Christians. The archbishop persuaded these monks to visit Grán under safe conduct from the king; which royal promise availed them as much as it had availed John Huss, for the Church had ways of disposing of her own disobedient underlings with which the Golden Bull could not interfere. A third monk, protected by the immediate presence of Count Pempflinger, delivered a series of popular lectures on Luther's theses in the Transylvanian capital itself. His zealous converts preached and catechised in the open air, in streets and market-places. When Corpus Christi day arrived, and the superb ceremonies of the festival invited all comers, many dissenting voices were heard. "These priests think God to be a child, whom they must carry about in their arms," said one. Disrespectful observations were made about the noonday candle-light of the processions and the mumbled music. The craft of the Church was in danger, by which she had her wealth.

The wisest of men hath written, "Woe unto thee, O land, when thy king is a child!" Louis of Hungary was only sixteen when he became the blind tool of the Romish hierarchy. A clever legate was sent to be his ecclesiastical tutor, even that Cardinal Cajétan who tried his hand with Luther and failed, but now he easily gained his point of having a murderous edict issued: "All Lutherans and those who favour them"—a sweeping clause, verily!—"shall have their property confiscated and be themselves punished with death, as heretics and foes of the most holy Virgin Mary."

How would that "blessed among women" be grieved if she could know the crimes that have been committed in her name! Not long afterward the pastor Nicolai, of a certain mining town in the mountains, being convicted of the above offences, was stabbed and burned near the castle of Dobrony, as a heretic "who had refused the Virgin Mary her due honour."

A worse edict was procured at the Diet of Bakosch next year: "All Lutherans shall be rooted out of the land, and wherever they are found, either by clergy or laymen, they may be seized and burned."

Hitherto, the chief burnings had been of books, but such fuel was too insensible to satisfy the enemies of the gospel. And again did God make the wrath of men to praise him by using the scourge of the Moslem sword to stay the persecutors.

CHAPTER VII.

MOHÄCS.

THE voyager up the Danube at this day pauses in his course to gaze at the great fortress of Peterwardein, which is the Gibraltar of Hungary. He sees a mighty rock fronted with bastions, long lines of curtain and half-moon batteries just revealing the iron lips of cannon, and wonders whether ever a foe captured the seemingly impregnable fastness. Solyman the Magnificent did capture the fortress in the year 1526, and in the pride of his achievements dictated a letter to King Louis, demanding tribute from him.

A little farther on the voyager passes the insignificant village of Mohäcs, with which name Europe once rang as with unexampled disaster. Louis of Hungary had gathered an army, helped by sixty thousand ducats from the pope, and the silver coffin of St. Gerhard melted down for the occasion, yet he could muster only twenty-seven thousand men, and no better general than an archbishop. He and they were all slain, for the Turks were fifteen to one. The ruby-hilted sword of the unfortunate Louis is yet to be seen in the palace of the Esterházy princes.

The issue of the battle had been foretold by one of the bishops present, who remarked, satirically, "Here go twenty-six thousand Hungarians, under the guidance of the Franciscan Tomory, as martyrs for the faith; and it would be highly desirable if at least the chancellor, who is acquainted with the pope, could be spared to go to Rome and have them all canonized!"

The triumphant Solyman marched to Ofen and burned the town. Long did literature mourn the destruction of the famous library gathered there by King Matthias Corvinus, containing forty thousand manuscript volumes; for he kept thirty secretaries constantly copying books which he borrowed from the universities and princes of other countries. The learned Brassican, who visited the library in its palmy days, wrote thus enthusiastically about it: "I have seen all these books. Do I call them books? So many treasures did I contemplate there! Who can believe what I felt at such a spectacle!" But now Solyman burned them all, and the glory of Corvinus and his kingdom was departed.

In the confusion consequent on this irruption of the Turks heresy was let alone. Who should be elected king—whether the native Hungarian, John Zapolya, or the German Ferdinand, brother of the emperor Charles V. and afterward king of the Romans—was a more interesting question than any theological one, even to the Church of Rome.

CHAPTER VIII.

QUEEN MARY OF HUNGARY.

FERDINAND was also brother to the widow of King Louis, and she supported his cause with all her power. This royal lady was not only a patron of the Reformers, having for her chaplain the devoted John Henkel, a friend of Erasmus, but she seems to have received the truth of God into her own heart. She always carried about with her a Latin Testament, full of annotations in her own writing; proving that she not only read the word, but sought to meditate upon and understand it. Luther wrote to her, saying he had "with great pleasure seen that she was a friend of the gospel;" and he sent her four psalms he had translated, and a hymn he had composed for her comfort ("Mag auf Unglück nicht wiederstehn").

Lying in the broad Danube at Buda are some beautiful islets, which have often been connected with Hungarian history; hoary ruins still remain to attest departed greatness. On one of these took place the parting of the youthful Queen Mary and her husband Louis, before he went to be slain at Mohäcs. They had been but a short time married, and they loved one another: more need not be said of the bitterness of the blow to her heart.

She was hated by the Romish party for her adherence to the Reformed doctrines; and now, that the protection of her husband was removed, the prelates, always noted for persecution of the weak, made her sharply feel their enmity. Her sorrowful spirit found utterance, amid all her state anxieties and personal trouble, in verses which have been translated thus:

"This is my strength, that well I know,
In weal or woe,
God's love the world must leave me:
God is not far, though hidden now:
He soon shall rise, and make them bow
Who of his word bereave me.

"Judge as ye will my cause this hour,
Yours is the power;
God bids me strive no longer:
I know what mightiest seems to-day
Shall pass away:
Time than your rule is stronger.

Th' Eternal Good I rather choose,
And fearless, all for this I lose:
God aid me thus to conquer!

"All hath its day, the proverb saith:
This is my faith,
Thou, Christ, wilt be beside me:
And look on all this pain of mine
As it were thine,
When sharpest woes betide me.
Must I then tread this path?—I yield;
World, as thou wilt! God is my shield,
And he will rightly guard me."

With this faith, as "an anchor of the soul, sure and steadfast," the widowed queen left Hungary and went to the court of her imperial brother, who did her much honour, and would not suffer her to be molested for religion's sake. She was present at the celebrated Diet of Augsburg (1530), where her heart must have echoed the Protestant Confession; and when Charles silenced all other Reformed preachers in attendance, her aforesaid chaplain, John Henkel, continued daily to expound the the word of God before her. Subsequently she was regent in the Low Countries, and showed her unfitness for the pope's purposes so markedly that his nuncio complained that "the queen did not cease on all occasions to show favour to the

Lutheran religion;" the special ground of which accusation was, that she had tried to throw a shield over the persecuted Protestants of France. And so she passed away from the history of Hungary, leaving that land of her brief wifehood rent in twain under rival kings and its capital possessed by the infidel.

CHAPTER IX.

RIVAL ROYAL PERSECUTORS.

THE crown had been elective in Hungary since 1301, when the line of the Magyar chief Arpad ceased. Strangely wild were the scenes that often took place at these royal elections, where a kingdom was the prize. Matthias Corvinus, the monarch of whom Hungarian history is proudest, was proclaimed by forty thousand soldiers standing on the frozen Danube beneath the terraced heights of Buda. At other times the Magyar nobility assembled on the Rákos Mezö, or field of Rákos, the great sandy plain outside Pesth, which is the modern suburb (across the Danube) of the grand old capital, Buda. Here they gathered, all armed and appointed for war, from the proudest magnate to the petty "sandalled" noble—a turbulent parliament, in sooth! Calmness in council, conjoined with a liability to sudden outbursts of violent feeling, is a characteristic of the Eastern races, to which belongs the Magyar: the latter occurred with more frequency than the former. At such a diet was the resolution carried by storms of acclamation in 1505 that for the future "no foreigner should be chosen king: a native Hungarian must wear the crown of Stephen," because the reigning monarch was that indolent Ladislaus, surnamed "Dobre," or "Very well," for the reason that to every request of every nature he was wont to reply this word, signifying that the petitioner might have it as he pleased; the king could not take the trouble of investigation or denial. His incapacity produced so much mischief (among others, severe persecutions of the Hussites, for Ladislaus could not find in his heart to deny the desires of the priests) that the diet, illogically tracing his moral weakness to his foreign blood, declared that in future a Hungarian only should rule over Hungary.

The person chiefly instrumental in obtaining this decree had a distant design upon the crown himself. He was voivode of Transylvania, John Zapolya by name; and when Solyman had left the country, recalled to Turkey by internal troubles, he was chosen king by a gathering of nobles three months after the battle of Mohäcs.

But Ferdinand of Austria was also chosen king by a Diet of Presburg; and in the very same cathedral which was signalized by the crowning of John in November, 1526, was Ferdinand crowned November, 1527, by the same archbishop. And now which of these rival monarchs would bid highest for the all-powerful support of the Church? He who persecuted best and most. John issued an edict against the Lutherans, threatening confiscation of goods if they did not return to Romanism. Some burnings took place with his royal sanction in the mining districts, where the shafts of the underground workings did duty, as once did the catacombs, in protecting the persecuted servants of God.

And Ferdinand, not to be behindhand, issued a much more elaborate proclamation from Buda as soon as he got possession, setting forth that "whoever mischievously and perseveringly holds and believes anything contrary to the twelve articles of our holy Christian faith, or contrary to the seven sacraments, shall be punished in his body and life. He shall lose his honours, and can never again be admitted to a place of trust. No one is bound to keep any contract with him or pay any debt. He has no right to buy or sell; no right to work at a trade or profession; he cannot make a will. A Roman Catholic father may disinherit a heretic son, and an orthodox son may dispossess a heretic father of his property."

Thus was "the commandment of God set at naught" by the evil counsellors of Ferdinand—the eternal commandments, written in nature as well as in revelation, by which men honour their parents; and another word of Christ was fulfilled when he said that the foes of his followers should be those of their own households. The decree put a premium upon filial disloyalty, and introduced the basest system of spying and informing into the closest relationships of life. It is well to know that an unchangeable Rome once approved such conduct.

Furthermore, the heaviest penalties were denounced against whoever should "despise or dishonour the eternal, pure, elect queen, the Virgin Mary, by saying, holding, writing, or preaching, that she was only a woman like other women on earth; that she is not the mother of God; that she did not ascend into heaven." Partaking of both bread and wine in the Lord's Supper was a crime to be also visited on the house in which such a deed took place: it was, "according to the royal pleasure, to be torn down, for an eternal testimony. Whoever mischievously holds that the mass has no merits for souls in purgatory shall be banished from the kingdom." All who received heretics into their houses were declared "*ipso facto* infamous," and deprived of the rights of citizens; any magistrates or judges who neglected to carry out the edict subjected their town to the loss of all its privileges. The informer respecting any of these offences should have the third of the confiscated property. And lest good Catholics should not be aware of their opportunities of enriching themselves at the expense of any Protestant friend or neighbour, the edict was directed to be solemnly read from every pulpit in Hungary at the festivals of Easter and Christmas.

Nevertheless, the truth spread and prospered. A great many of the magnates declared for the Reformation. In Transylvania the municipal authorities of the capital, Hermannstadt, ordered all monks and nuns to leave the city and take with them their possessions, or else to "give up their mummeries and live according to the gospel." This produced a great change, for monasteries are the pope's fortresses sprinkled through a land. Except for the threatening yet protecting shadow of Sultan Solyman, the Transylvanians scarce dared thus defy the Romish hierarchy; but he came back to Hungary in that year, 1529, to help his ally John Zapolya, and held a divan at Buda, where he bound himself never to forsake that king, even to the cost of his own empire. Ferdinand had retired into Austria and was presiding at the German Diet of Spires, and so the rival persecutions were stayed for the present.

CHAPTER X.

THE HUNGARIAN LUTHER.

AT Buda, among all the palaces, were many prisons, which in those ages were too often even the basement story of palaces. The most celebrated was the Czonka-Torony, or Mutilated Tower, so called because never finished. It was mined with subterranean passages and dungeons, and here the kings of Hungary cast any unfortunates that had incurred their displeasure.

A poor blacksmith was shut up in one of these prisons while John Zapolya held the town—his offence, having lamed the king's favourite horse while putting on a shoe; and John, who was no cruel tyrant, but merely a passionate Hungarian magnate, vowed he should die for the deed, as he was merely a serf without civil rights. And while the unhappy artisan lay thus in terror of his life, expecting every day the headsman's summons, another man was thrown into the same prison, who also had committed an action deemed worthy of death. But whereas the blacksmith was in fear and sorrow, the other prisoner seemed contented and happy. He had holy words of praise on his lips oftentimes, and he laboured to impart to his fellow-prisoner somewhat of the same divine consolation that filled his own soul.

So it came to pass that when the king forgot his anger and sent to release the blacksmith, he would not go, because, he said, he believed as Matthew Devay believed, and whatever was to be the Lutheran pastor's fate he would share. John Zapolya was moved. This strange contagion of faith —what could it mean? He obeyed a benevolent impulse and ordered the freedom of both.

What! set free the man who had lived so long at Wittemberg with the pestilent arch-heretic Martin Luther, even dwelling in his family and eating at his table, till he was as much imbued with heresy as his master?—the man who had preached in Transylvania under protection of the powerful heretic noble Caspar Dragfij, and had drawn away many other nobles to embrace his opinions—nay, who had even taught certain villages so effectually that they separated from the holy mother Church? But John Zapolya would have his own way this time, and Matthew Devay

Matthew Devay in Prison.

escaped the fangs of the ecclesiastical courts through a royal whim of good-nature.

He then tried the dominions of the other Hungarian king, Ferdinand, and settled as pastor at a town in Upper Hungary. Not the danger he had escaped nor any sharper lesson could make him hold his peace when the truth or God was in question. He exposed the abuses of the Romish Church with such powerful eloquence that the monks of that district felt "all hope of their gains was gone." The local authorities were all in his favour, for Lutheranism prevailed immensely among the middle classes and even among the nobility—we shall find in a few years hence only three families of importance among the magnates or peers of Hungary that were not Protestant—so that a complaint to the magistrates would be useless. They carried their accusation to the royal ear itself, and Ferdinand was the brother of that emperor who spent all his life trying to force men by fire and sword into uniformity of religion—an effort which the discordant time-pieces at the convent of Yuste taught him in his old age was utterly vain. Ferdinand proved his pious zeal to please the Church by at once ordering Devay in custody to Vienna.

The Austrian capital was an ominous place of

trial for a Reformer. Caspar Tauber had been burned there only a few years since, and a bitter enemy to the gospel was Dr. John Faber, royal councillor, to whose examination the Hungarian pastor was referred. He had been the most active member of an inquisitorial commission sent through Austria, Styria and Carinthia to see how far the decrees against the Lutherans had been carried out and to enforce greater stringency.

Two years was the Hungarian pastor kept in prison, uncertain of the issue of his case: by such discipline God educates his soldiers of the cross. Think what it must be to have the fiery death before one's eyes as a probably approaching fate for twenty-four long months! Then King Ferdinand interfered—unaccountably, as men would say—and Matthew Devay was again liberated.

Ferdinand's character has much puzzled some historians. At times he seemed to favour the Reformation, but at others he seemed afraid to offend Rome. Of a naturally good disposition, without any fixed principles and without personal religion, he allowed himself to be carried away by impulses, and had neither power nor wish to form a decided judgment on some of the most important points. A double-minded man, saith the word of God, is unstable in all his ways. Some represent him as a friend of the Reformers—others as their bitterest foe, who spared the Protestants only from political motives. The truth seems to be that his own character was changeable and undecided.

It is not strange to find him, after this experience of Austrian rule, going back into the dominions of John Zapolya, Ferdinand's rival. Protestantism could not be so systematically crushed here. Many nobles and princes received him joyfully into their houses and castles as he travelled from place to place, an itinerant preacher with the good news of God upon his lips and in his heart. He lived after the manner of an apostle, and was blessed with an apostle's joys in seeing many souls turned from darkness to light, and whole districts casting off the yoke of Rome. He was anxious for the translation of the Scriptures and their wide diffusion, which he knew could alone build up the new converts in their most holy faith; and he worked at rendering the epistles of Paul into the Magyar tongue, which was accomplished and the book printed in 1533. It was dedicated to a noble lady, mother of one of the greatest Hungarian magnates, Perényi, who with his three sons had embraced the truth, having first learned it at the court of Queen Mary. Certainly God has honoured women to do much in the Reformation cause.

The four Gospels were published at Pesth in 1536, and the same year we find Matthew Devay going to Wittemberg again. He desired to refresh his soul at the fountain-head of the Reformation; and what must have been the mutual communings of those devoted men who risked all things for the love of Jesus Christ! Kindred faith and kindred suffering on its account form the closest of spirit-bonds. Again he lived in Luther's house and imbibed the wisdom that fell from the lips of that very clear-sighted man; and so much of his energetic and fearless spirit seemed to descend upon Devay that he has been called the Hungarian Luther.

He wrote an account of his Viennese imprisonment and examinations before the councillor Faber, which was printed at Nuremberg, and had large circulation in an age that abounded with such literature, because abounding in the tyranny that caused it. We can imagine the Wittemberg doctors eagerly gaining all the news about Hungary from the Magyar pastor, and hearing of the persecution that still raged in certain districts, and would have raged far worse had King Ferdinand's decrees been properly obeyed. But, thanks to the bulwark of the nobility's privileges, both royal and ecclesiastical tyranny had bounds they dared not pass.

Another magnate protected Devay when he went back to his own country. There is a long lake, called the Balaton or Platten See, communicating with the Danube in Lower Hungary, on the margin of which the magnate Nadasdy had his great estates, and here he sheltered various gospel preachers in open defiance of king and clergy. He even sheltered them from each other when they had differences which ripened into the Lutheran and Zwinglian divisions, among which Devay sided with Zwingle, and became a believer in the purely memorial nature of the Lord's Supper. The largest part of the Hungarian Protestant Church ultimately agreed with him. The Swiss Confession was laid before a synod of pastors, at Débrécsin, in 1557, and signed by all.

In the county of Presburg stands a free city, called Tyrnau, where Devay laboured for a long time. Once it had been called Little Rome, so zealous were its people for the old Church, but their zeal was soon transferred to the opposite side, under the earnest preaching of the Hungarian Luther. Travellers still visit with interest its round Byzantine Dom-Kirche, or cathedral, six hundred years old, crowned with zinc-covered domes and lined with statues of brave knights who fought the Turks, and bishops who waxed decrepit in enjoyment of the see. There is also a sumptuous chapel of the Virgin, with altar of beaten silver and trappings to match about the chief idol itself. Yet was this cathedral for some time in possession of the Protestants, and used solely for their worship, because nearly all the citizens had been converted under the preaching of Devay and his colleagues. The Jesuits had to build another church for themselves.

CHAPTER XI.

FERDINAND AND THE HERETIC.

AFTER Devay had been sent prisoner from his pastorate in Upper Hungary to Vienna, another man was raised up to feed the sheep of Christ in that place. His name was Stephen Szantai: he was noted for learning and for courage. The monks found they had not gained much by the removal of Devay. His successor was not a bit frightened, and declared against their superstitions as boldly as Devay had done. The stop of the strong hand must be put to him and his sermons.

Three bishops complained of him to Ferdinand. The humour for a public discussion seized the royal mind. He had not so much need of the Church's aid in political matters just now, because he had concluded a peace with his rival, John Zapolya, by which each was to hold what he had during life, and at the death of John the kingdom was to pass to Ferdinand; so he did not mind vexing the hierarchy a little. He appointed that a public disputation should be held between the accusing monks and Stephen Szantai, the accused pastor.

The king chose two umpires of unimpeachable quality, who were to take notes and present their decision for the royal approval. The bishop of Grosswardein sent his ablest theologian to aid the monks. A vast crowd of people came to listen, some from great distances, day after day. They heard much noise on the part of the monks, who seemed to think that speaking all at once would crush the solitary heretic under a weight of words, if not of arguments. To his help came a Lutheran physician, a man not trained to debate, but nevertheless able to handle the sword of the Spirit with effect, and showed how inefficient were their attempts to put down truth by clamour. The umpires, being men really void of partisanship, reported to the king in favour of Stephen Szantai, who had grounded all his statements upon the word of God itself, while the monks had brought forward only traditions and the reasonings of schoolmen. But, being men of prudence likewise, the umpires added that if they dared state this publicly they were undone, "while if we condemn

Szantai, we act contrary to truth and justice, and cannot escape God's righteous retribution."

Ferdinand was much struck by their decision, but he saw the wisdom of temporizing as fully as they did, because neither felt the influence of divine truth upon their hearts. He received the bishops and monks very blandly when they waited on him that same afternoon to demand the burning of Stephen Szantai. Justly they believed the fagot a more powerful argument than the old wives' fables of their traditions.

"Your majesty has acted contrary to our wish in granting this despicable heretic a public hearing, that others might suck in his poison. Our holy father the pope will be under little obligation to your majesty for this: there is no need of discussing what the Church has already condemned. One should not even remain in the presence of such a miserable apostate. We demand that he be brought here and burned, as a warning to others."

The bishop of Grosswardein had spoken rather too strongly for royal ears, and Ferdinand answered with dignity that he would allow no man to be put to death until proved guilty of a capital crime. "Bring forward your charge and he shall be judged according to law."

"Is it not enough," cried Statilius, bishop of Stuhlweissenberg—"is it not enough that he declares the mass to be an invention of the devil—that he demands both bread and wine at the Eucharist for all, while Christ appointed the full sacrament only for the priests?"

Whereupon the king turned upon the prelate and demanded whether he recognized the Greek Church as a true Church.

"Yea, your majesty," was the answer, as he expected.

"And yet the Greeks take communion in both kinds as taught by their holy patriarchs, Chrysostom and Cyril. If they do it without sin, why may not we? They never had the mass, and do well without it: why could not we also?"

Royal logic need not be very cogent to be convincing, but there was such common sense here that the bishops looked at one another, attempting no answer. Rage filled their hearts notwithstanding. "If your majesty do not grant our wish, we shall find other means to dispose of this vulture," exclaimed the bishop of Grosswardein in a passion.

Ferdinand replied, temperately: "The facts of the case shall be investigated, for it does not become my royal dignity to punish innocence. God would not hold me guiltless."

Late at night he sent for the persecuted preacher to a private audience. "What, then, is really the doctrine you teach?" he asked.

"Most gracious prince, it is no new invention, but divine grace has taught it to me," replied Szantai. "It is the doctrine of the prophets and apostles, and of our Lord Jesus Christ himself." And he told in the ears of Ferdinand and the princes present the blessed truth of the gospel.

The king was moved by his earnestness. Perhaps, like Felix, he thought that at a more convenient season he would turn his attention to these things. Such seasons come seldomer to kings than to common men! At all events, Ferdinand resolved to save him.

"My dear brother Stephen," thus the king of the Romans addressed the obscure Protestant pastor, "you and I are both ruined if we adhere to these doctrines. We commit the cause to God, who knows the right, but you must leave my land or the bishops will have your life. Go and put yourself under the protection of the voivode of Transylvania, where you may freely profess your opinions." He gave Szantai some handsome presents, and sent him away by night under a guard into the dominions of his rival, John Zapolya. And thus was it proved that "the king's heart is in the hand of the Lord, as the rivers of water: he turneth it whithersoever he will."

For it was directly contrary to the usual course of Ferdinand's conduct that he should befriend a heretic. He was commonly a ready tool in priestly hands for state reasons. Not long afterward he issued an edict from Nuremberg, giving the clergy fullest powers of persecution. Also he wrote from Prague to the Hungarian vice-palatine (Francis von Reva, himself in correspondence with Luther), threatening him with that terror of courtiers, loss of royal favour, if he did not stringently execute the laws against heretics. The magnate Perényi was cast into prison, ostensibly because he was suspected of treasonable designs, but really because he upheld the Lutherans with all his power.

When these facts are remembered, the interference of King Ferdinand to save Stephen Szantai's life appears more like a miraculous interposition of that Lord whose "eyes run to and fro in the earth, to show himself strong in behalf" of his people, than an event of his ordinary providence. Did

Ferdinand recollect a deathbed of which he had been witness not long previously, when the dying man (his own chaplain and a Spaniard) assured him that Luther taught the truth, against which he had bitterly opposed? Conscience spoke with the voice of conviction in that dread hour, and told Ferdinand that this confessor had all his life been leading his soul astray.

CHAPTER XII.

PLAGUE COLUMNS.

THE most tolerant people in Europe at that age were the Turks. While Ferdinand and John Zapolya persecuted the Protestants by turns to please the Church, Solyman and his pashas treated both religious parties with a lofty indifference; so that when the recorder of a certain Hungarian city brought a large present to the Moslem general, requesting that he would be good enough—in virtue of the bribe—to banish all Lutherans and Calvinists, the turbaned infidel made close inquiry into the matter, pocketed the present, threatened to slay the recorder, and published a decree that Luther's doctrines should everywhere be freely preached.

Traces of lengthened Turkish rule abound throughout Hungary to this day. Sometimes they are the ruins of a useful erection, as the baths over the sulphur springs at Buda, or the aqueduct conveying the medicated waters of Mehadia to the frontier town of Orsova, where a pasha dwelt; but more often they are mere remnants of ravage. Travellers describe the strange underground villages to be met with in some districts most exposed to incursion—human burrows roofed with straw and devoid of light, except what enters by door and chimney. These could not be so utterly destroyed by the Moslem cavalry as more pretentious villages, neither were they so observable from a distance. But what a vivid idea they present of the hunted condition of the people!

The Turks brought into Hungary, and left there behind them, one fearful visitant—the plague. In most towns of note are found those curious pillars called plague columns, being obelisks or spires built as praying places for priests and people when the scourge was apprehended. Presburg, the city of the diet, has two of these pillars situated very prominently, and profusely decorated with images of the Virgin and saints, gilded at the summit, and used now as stations for the pause of religious processions. They might indeed serve as remembrancers for the gratitude of the present generation, favoured by the total absence of both rapacious Turk and the ravaging plague which has ever followed his conquering step like a black shadow. An artist of that period erecting a plague column at Kremnitz, carved on his sandstone pedestal the appropriate bas-relief of Aaron standing with his flaming censer between the dead and the living — "making atonement for the people."

Buda was held by the Turks all through Ferdinand's reign, and for more than a century afterward. They were not then "the sick man" of Europe, but a mighty power continually looming from the East like a thunder-cloud, especially to papal apprehensions. All beyond the river Theiss and through Transylvania and Wallachia, heretic preachers and people abounded, on whom the pope himself dared not set a finger. A run across the frontier into the countries of the Crescent gave liberty of conscience; and the fruit of Turkish tolerance is visible even now in the widespread Protestantism of those outlying provinces. Few of the gentry or lower nobles are Roman Catholics. The mass profess the faith of the Augsburg Confession, and are as strongly attached to their creed as are Englishmen.

CHAPTER XIII.

THE HUNGARIAN BIBLE.

THE year 1541 was signalized by the publication of a complete Hungarian Testament, translated mainly by the pastor, John Sylvester, and dedicated in Latin to the sons of the king, Maximilian and Ferdinand. They patronized it as a literary effort more than as an engine of Reformation, for statesmen thought to be politic in encouraging the Magyar language.

We have before intimated that this is one of the strangest tongues spoken on European soil. It is an importation from the steppes of Tartary—east of the Volga live tribes who would understand its phrases. Modern philologists call it one of the Turanian (from *tura*, swiftness of a horseman, to express nomadic nature) or agglutinative languages, whereas our English is inflectional. A mark of difference striking every ear is, that a man's Christian name is set after his surname—thus, Szantai Stephen. While other European languages were cultivated and had some species of literature, Hungarian, from its total want of affinity with the Latin or any of the dialects formed from Latin, was considered barbarous, and no man wrote in it. But for popular purposes the use of the Magyar tongue was indispensable—the people's heart was to be reached through it. Therefore a Hungarian version of the Scriptures had been more than once attempted by those who believed that "the entrance of God's word gives light and understanding to the simple." We have named the obscure monk who laboured at it for nearly twenty years of seclusion in a mountain hermitage, yet grew not weary of the task.

The Servians, lying south of Hungary, had got a Bible in 1493. The Hungarians had not theirs, completed by the pastor Caroli, for near a century afterward; it bears date 1589.

Both clergy and laity had zealously cultivated a sort of bad Latin for a long period: ever since the time of Stephen, the canonized king, it was supremely vulgar to use Hungarian. But a living idiom is not so easily killed by a dead one, though even now travellers are sometimes surprised to find even the waiters at remote inns able to converse in the language of the Vulgate. And when the earliest Reformers wrote so much in Latin, their productions found the wider and readier audience throughout Hungary, among the educated classes, who accordingly proved the staunchest advocates of the Protestant religion.

The translator of the New Testament, John Sylvester, had been recommended to the protection of the Palatine Nádasdy by a letter from Melancthon. Such credentials were a necessary part of the equipment of evangelists in that age; and in most of them it could be said, as by the council of apostles at Jerusalem, that the bearers were "men who had hazarded their lives for the name of our Lord Jesus Christ."

CHAPTER XIV.

MELANCTHON'S LETTERS.

THIS gentlest of the German Reformers seems to have been regarded by Hungarian Christians as a sort of metropolitan. Naturally they looked to Wittemberg and the German Church for encouragement and example; upon Luther and his friends fell, as of yore upon Paul, "the care of all the churches." Crowds of young men went to study divinity under the greatest master of that heavenly science then on earth; among them many native Hungarians, who, after a course of theological instruction, were ordained and sent back to preach the gospel in their own land.

Melancthon never set foot in Hungary. But from his student's cell in Wittemberg he was able largely to influence the religious movements of its people by means of his letters. Not only to the Protestant pastors did he write, but to the magnates and lesser nobles who favoured the Reformation. The persecuted Prince Perényi was comforted in his prison by such apostolic epistles, exhorting him to bear all for the sake of Christ, who was able so richly to reward him.

In 1549, Ferdinand sent two royal commissioners to inquire into the religious state of Upper Hungary; in other words, to discover how far Protestantism had displaced Romanism, and to organize a more effectual crushing system. When the first fright was over, the pastors took courage and shrank not from the enemy's investigation, but presented the famous Pentapolitan or Five-Cities' Confession, containing twenty articles of faith. "It was nothing else than an extract from the Augsburg Confession, drawn up in Melancthon's soothing style;" and such was the effect of the soft but firm answer, that the king allowed those five towns still to enjoy their privileges, and committed no act of tyranny at that time.

Again, we find Melancthon acting as metropolitan in the case of the pastor Lauterwaldt, who was guilty of preaching error. A synod of the neighbouring clergy forwarded an appeal to Melancthon, asking whether it were right that Lauterwaldt should affirm that a sinner is saved jointly by his own works and the blood of Jesus Christ;

and the Reformer wrote that the man teaching such falsehood should be deposed. The very essence of the gospel, that for which they had come out from Rome and braved all her terrors, lay involved in the question, Is salvation of God's free grace alone?

One of the last public acts of Melancthon was to ordain a Hungarian pastor whom he had been educating in the faith. This Reformer had that strange, attractive power, divinely bestowed upon some men, by which they draw hearts to them and retain love always. His pupils never forgot his affectionate care, nor the gentleness that had borne with faults and magnified excellences; they gave him far more than the common regard of scholars for a teacher, and when he died the mourning was widespread. Hearts ached for him in the Black Forest and by the Swedish seas, in crowded French towns and upon the steppes of Hungary. One Leonard Stöckel, rector of the high school in the Protestant town of Bartfield, was lying sick when he received a letter from Melancthon, and the messenger who brought it had also the sad news of Melancthon's death. The Hungarian pastor never recovered that blow; and whereas there were some questions in the letter respecting the state of the

Church and such-like matters, "I shall answer him in heaven," quoth the pastor, "for soon I shall follow my beloved teacher." And so he also died.

CHAPTER XV.

CONFERENCES AND CONCESSIONS.

IT seems strange to us Protestants of the nineteenth century how much was hoped from a general council in the sixteenth. The eyes of all Europe were on the long-promised gathering of ecclesiastics, who should by their wisdom heal the vast breach in that Church which ought to be the seamless robe of Christ. Ferdinand, king of Hungary and of the Romans, heir-apparent to the imperial crown of Germany, was one of the most ardent believers in the Council of Trent and all that it should accomplish. He desired his deputies, two Hungarian bishops, to demand reformation of morals and of faith as the first object of the council's efforts. He wanted to have fewer cardinals, fewer indulgences, no "religion of money," and that hitherto unknown anomaly, a humble-minded pope. As concessions to the Lutheran party, he asked for the abolition of fast-days and the granting of the cup to the laity. But these alterations would not touch "the weightier matters of the law"—"the word of God only, the work of Christ only."

Ferdinand sent a bishop to Venice to see how the priests of the Greek Church managed their religious services, and especially the Lord's Supper. He was most anxious that some compromise should be authorized by the council—some comprehensive scheme which might draw into uniformity of system all the dissenters of his dominions. But his Hungarian deputies at Trent soon discovered that all attempts at reformation would be vain. Bishop Dudith wrote thus to his royal master:

"As the votes are estimated by number and not by weight"—of character or influence—"the pope can send hundreds or even thousands to vote against the well-disposed party. We see every day hangers-on at the Roman court, and beardless bishops, young men who have lost their property and their character, coming to Trent in order to vote as pleases the pope. What these men want in learning or intelligence is fully compensated by their impudence. The affairs of the Church are here regulated by puppets which are moved by foreign hands, like the fabled images of Dædalus.

The Holy Spirit has nothing to do with the council. Here are simply human schemes to aggrandize Rome. The spirit which is represented as guiding the meetings comes in the postman's bag from Rome, and must wait at every swollen river in the road till the waters abate!"

This was tolerably sharp satire from an episcopal pen. We are not amazed to learn that the writer subsequently became a Lutheran, resigned his see of Funfkirchen and his office as an imperial ambassador, and took refuge in Poland, only three years after his experiences at the infallible council.

How that council ended all the world knows. Its unscriptural decisions were defended with anathema—its last utterance was curses. More than ever was the breach in the seamless robe widened. Pius the Fourth's foundationless creed was Trent's legacy to the Church.

Ferdinand, king of Hungary, remonstrated. To please him, the pope consented to revise the decisions of infallibility and render harmless in Hungary what would anywhere else ruin a soul—viz., communion in both kinds. His Holiness addressed a papal bull to the archbishop of Grán, prince-primate of the kingdom, authorizing him and his priests to give the cup to the laity. The first communicant in this form was Ferdinand himself. He was so charmed with the concession that he struck a medal, as if he had gained a victory, which truly he had in some sort. On the obverse his own bust, with the encircling motto in German, "Giebt dem Kaiser was des Kaiser's ist," signifying, "Render unto Cæsar what is Cæsar's;" on the reverse a cup above the word "Oratio"—"prayer," and with the encircling motto, "Giebt Gott was Gottes ist"—"Give God what is God's."

The expression of triumph was premature, so far as regarded the effect of this notable concession. Such crumbs could not satisfy men who had sat at the full table of God's free grace and been nourished on the sincere milk and strong meat of the word. It is to be doubted if granting the cup brought back a score of the recusants.

The covenant, as a device for affording stability to a religious body, was not an invention peculiar to Scottish Reformers. We find it in Hungary, 1561, when the troops, nobles and citizens of the town of Erlau bound themselves by an oath to uphold the truth taught them from the word of God; and all who could write signed a confession of faith corresponding chiefly with that of the

Helvetic Church. This time-honoured document is still preserved in a library at Presburg. And when the leaders of the movement were charged with high treason, and arraigned before a court of justices by the artifices and misrepresentations of the hierarchy, they declared that obedience to their king ceased with civil affairs and that their souls were to obey none but God—that Ezra and Nehemiah had made the same sort of league for the preservation of the truth and the glory of God. Their undaunted demeanour and the weight of their words influenced their judges to an acquittal of the charge.

On the whole, the hand of the persecutor in Hungary was very much stayed during this century, while Italy, Spain, the Netherlands, and for a time England, were actually reeking with the blood of the martyrs of Jesus. Oppression there was in abundance, but judicial murders at stake or scaffold were fewer than in most other lands where the struggle between light and darkness was progressing.

So much freedom was exercised by Reformed pastors that they held conferences about the constitution of their Church, and gradually built up its system according to their experience of its working. They abolished the confessional, arranged for the support of the clergy in poor parishes—for all existing ecclesiastical endowments were grasped firmly by the Romish party; they tried to produce uniformity of opinion about the Lord's Supper, where the Lutheran saw the body of Christ and bread, but the Zwinglian saw only bread; they decided that in places where altars existed they should be allowed to remain, though no fresh one should be erected or rebuilt—a resolve savouring of the moderation of men who were in no danger. Again, we read of a conference at Hermannstadt, the capital of Transylvania, where Paul Viener was chosen first superintendent of the Reformed Church, and a number of evangelical ministers were ordained by imposition of hands.

CHAPTER XVI.

THE DIET OF EDENBERG.

THIS free city of Edenberg was one of the earliest where the Reformation struck root. In the ancient accounts of the municipal treasurer, date 1525, is found the following entry: "Monday after New Year's day, to the hangman for burning Lutheran books, 1 d, d." This was before the battle of Mohäcs and the irruption of the Turks had cooled the ardour of the persecuting Romish clergy, and prevented their following up fires of books with fires consuming human beings.

Young men went into Germany to learn at the feet of the fathers of the Reformation, and came back, after the soundest theologic education, imbued with knowledge as well as with zeal of the first order. Rapidly the doctrines of the Bible won the hearts of the people, and spread through the district to the neighbouring fortress of Guns. Here the inhabitants declared in a body for the

Reformers, and Zwingle's views in particular; and considering the churches as built for popular use by their forefathers, and not to be shrines of an extinct idolatry, they adapted them to the new worship. In 1554 the last Roman Catholic priest left the city, because the last Romanist had been converted to Protestantism. Fairly beaten out of the field was the infallible Church.

The greatest pride of the Hungarian freeman is his national Diet, which he can point to as the bulwark of liberty for seven centuries past. Only five years later than the first real Parliament in England, was the first real representative Diet of Hungary held on the field of Rákos, outside Pesth. Since then, the rulers of Hungary have been obliged to seek the sanction of Diets for every action of importance. Ferdinand summoned one to meet at Edenberg in 1553, with a view to settling religious differences. And while the earliest Parliament of Mary Tudor was allowing her to burn heretics at will, this Hungarian parliament upheld the Reformation and freedom of conscience gallantly against all the weight of the court and Austrian faction. A law was proposed to forbid the printing and distribution of Protestant books; the hereditary and elected legislators of Hungary declared for freedom of the press, and would have none of the shackles of bigotry.

Even in "Cæsar's household" were Protestants found at this Diet. The palatine, who is vicegerent of the king, the master of the ceremonies at court, the colonel of the life-guards, were all men who had cast off allegiance to the pope. Likewise a large majority of the magnates or peers of Hungary, and all the magistrates of the city.

The burgomaster having given himself to the cause of the truth, thought it a less thing to give of his possessions; and he allotted even his garden for the building of an evangelical high school wherein to educate young Protestants. The whole town council united in an invitation to Simon Gerengel, who had been a priest in Lower Austria, to become pastor in Edenberg. He was a miserably poor exile at the time he received their letter, which was to him a veritable message from God. He had been led by Melancthon's "Common Places" to the Bibles, and thence had learned to distinguish what he calls "the horribly soul-destroying errors of Popery;" in consequence of which discernment he was thrown into prison at Salzburg for above three years; where so close was his confinement that though his aged mother came afoot more than two hundred miles for the purpose of seeing him, she was not allowed to do so. "Here I lie," he wrote—"here I lie day after day, month after month, year after year, till it please the Lord Jesus to set me free."

Simon Gerengel had further work to do for his Master on earth, and so he escaped a martyr's death at that time; in obscure and wretched poverty and opprobrium he and his family lived for some years, until the call to Edenberg reached him. Here he did such good service to the growing Church that multitudes were added "of such as should be saved;" and the crowning accession was the chief Romanist priest of the town.

Edenberg was a stronghold of Protestantism during that century. The school built in the good burgomaster's garden became a centre of light and its professors ardent Reformers. Five Hungarian preachers filled the pulpits of the town. Gradually the popish observances which clung round the youth of Protestantism dropped off. German hymns were sung at the services instead of Latin; funeral processions lit with huge tapers were abolished. As this improvement aimed a blow at the sacerdotal pocket, we find that a warm-tempered priest retaliated by publicly boxing the ears of the rector of the college who had originated it. Only conscious and enraged weakness would have taken such petty revenge; nothing of the kind occurred as long as fagot or headsman's sword could be used by priestly hands.

Names which have survived that period in Edenberg are those of the ministers Stephen Beytha and Michael Starinus. The former filled a greater space in the world while he lived, being preacher forty-five years in a prominent position, but he left no such enduring work as the latter to follow him, and by which Michael Starinus, "being dead, yet speaketh." This pastor translated the Psalms of David into Hungarian verse, and thereby furnished the Church with her songs of praise even to this day. There could scarce be loftier usefulness than that which has made the hearts of generations flow forth in praise to the Most High.

CHAPTER XVII.

THE FIRST MAXIMILIAN.

HE was a gentle prince, considering the race from which he sprang and the school in which he had been trained. Two of the cruelest persecutors of the age were his uncle and cousin. Yet even before the death of his father Ferdinand he had showed some Protestant tendencies and kept a Lutheran for his chaplain. State-craft stepped in and compelled him to conceal his tolerance; the Jesuits got round his wife and made her a bigot who embittered his home. Obliged to send away his Protestant chaplain—for princes are anything but the freest agents—he addressed him in these words: "Be of good courage, dear Pfauser; the service of God must not yield to the commandments of men." The chaplain had refused compliance with Rome.

It was in 1564 that Ferdinand, who had worn the crown of Hungary for thirty-eight years, was succeeded by his son Maximilian. Almost at once he interfered to protect the Protestants from the prince-primate, who had sent an order to Presburg that all heretical books should be collected and destroyed, likewise that all Reformed preachers should be banished. The citizens appealed to the king. At the same time came another appeal from the people of Schemnitz, chief of the mining towns in Northern Hungary. On them the prince-primate had thought to force the Jesuits as religious teachers, and threatened the severest punishment to the magistrates, because they reminded him that they adhered to the Augsburg Confession of Faith. Freedom of conscience he could not brook, and they were not willing to listen to the voice of any of Rome's charmers, and especially of those Jesuits, whose principal was a divine that had earned for himself the title of the Austrian hound (Canis Austriacus), by reason of his keen scent after heretics. It was a dismal play upon his name, Peter Canisius. The king heard the appeal of his mining towns, and wrote to the primate that he should "cease from disturbing the evangelical clergy—that he should consider the times and take heed he did not destroy more than he built up." And here, among the slag and silver of the mines, Hungarian

Protestantism has still a stronghold, thanks to the wise toleration of the First Maximilian.

He was anxious for compromise, like his father; he did his best to compass abolition of clerical celibacy, which he saw to be the root of many evils. And even if the Reformed and Roman churches could never be fused into one mass of uniformity again, why might they not exist side by side? True, there was a section of the Protestants that scarcely his liberality could endure—those called by the Romanists the Sacramentarian party, otherwise Zwinglians. He would not permit the ministers who adhered to the Swiss confession of faith to hold a synod at Edenberg; whence it will be seen that his royal toleration only went a certain length; he was resolved his subjects should still believe in the real presence, or in that slightly altered edition of the dogma set forth by the Lutherans.

War with the Turks was a necessary condition of the reign of every Hungarian king, and Maximilian had his share. The general of his army, Lazarus Schwend, was a Lutheran, and brought evangelical preachers in his train wherever he went. His ideas of toleration were as limited as his master's, for when a certain pastor was convicted of holding Socinian views, he threw him into prison and set him free only on recantation. Lazarus Schwend's successor was also a zealous Protestant.

Under such patronage the churches prospered. Stephen Szegedinus was a distinguished pastor of the time; one hundred and twenty congregations were under his superintendence in a single narrow district of Hungary, on the banks of the rapid Save. When sixty years old, he held a public discussion with a learned monk in Pesth, and came off victorious because authority was not permitted to crush truth.

Pope Gregory, who had lately sung Te Deum for the vast crime of St. Bartholomew's day, could not persuade the king of Hungary to persecute his Protestant subjects. The legate and bishops were weary of remonstrating against the latitude allowed the Reformed preachers, and of Maximilian's quiet reply that he would inquire into any case where their liberty of speech was abused.

The Jesuit Mitterdorfer says, "Maximilian gave full evidence of being a Roman Catholic prince." The very assertion shows there was some doubt on the subject. History relates that he dismissed a chaplain (once a Lutheran) who had sought to signalize his apostasy by a bitter attack on Protestantism, and so grave were the doubts of the Sorbonne respecting his orthodoxy that the honours customarily paid to deceased emperors and kings by that body were refused him. In 1576 he left the Hungarian crown to his son Rudolph, who was in character almost his exact opposite.

CHAPTER XVIII.

FORMAL SEPARATION FROM ROME.

CITIES, congregations, pastors, even private persons, had for years back been putting forth confessions of faith, agreeing in the main with that of Augsburg or of the Swiss Reformers. We read how Jehoiakim Brandenburg, chaplain of the German cavalry at Raab, thought it necessary to print and publish the articles of his belief, owing to the aspersions of his enemies. He announced also that he would preach in the open air at eight different stations upon these truths of his creed, as the use of a consecrated building was denied him.

One reason of the frequency of these confessions of faith was the spread of heterodox doctrines through Hungary. Unitarians and Socinians became very numerous, and true believers wished to have the world know that they had no sympathy with such as denied the divinity of our Lord Jesus Christ. For Rome was very ready to make this heresy of individuals a cause for persecuting the whole Church.

Notwithstanding all the confessions, Rome pretended to consider the Lutherans only a sect within her fold and still amenable to her discipline. This was the assumption necessary for persecution, that they were children — disobedient children — who needed chastisement. The bishop of Csanad wrote to the recusant twenty-four towns of Zip's country, saying he would soon visit them as their spiritual father, "armed with power to restore wanderers." Everybody knew what this meant. He summoned all the Protestant clergy to attend his synod, as well as the Romanists, and ominously added that he would purge his diocese.

Regular payment of church dues was also demanded, and in many Protestant communities yielded as an unjust tax, for peace' sake; until, in the year 1573, the aforesaid bishop of Csanad, who seems to have been especially unfortunate in the assertions of his authority, demanding his episcopal fees from the Reformed in his diocese, received instead a confession of faith, wherein their renunciation of his spiritual government was conveyed as follows:

"The Church is the visible body of those who

hear and believe the gospel, and among whom the sacraments are administered according to Christ's appointment. The Spirit of God works in these to renew their minds by his appointed means, but there are many in the visible Church whose minds are not yet renewed. Those pastors who falsify the Word, administer the sacraments according to Christ's intention and kill the saints — such are not the Church of God; but, as the Lord says, 'they are of their father the devil.'"

Whether the bishop recognized the likeness of his order in the last sentence cannot be known, but under the mild Maximilian he was obliged to simulate meekness before the affront. It was the beginning of the formal separation from Rome.

CHAPTER XIX.

TROUBLOUS TIMES.

PHILIP THE SECOND of Spain was no amiable character, and formed upon his model was his cousin Rudolph of Hungary. Only circumstances kept the latter from being as cruel a persecutor as the former, but he had just as implicit submission to the Roman Church, and was a tyrant of the same suspicious stamp, with his tyranny at the beck of the pope. And so days of peace for the Hungarian Reformers were ended.

Not that any sweeping persecution could be attempted: the ever-watchful Diet, wherein the upper chamber of magnates were nearly all Protestants, guarded well the liberties of the land. Congregations and pastors must be attacked in detail and under various pretexts harassed. A grand pretext was given by the introduction of the Gregorian calendar. The mass of Protestants could not possibly see the improvement in their reckoning of time, but regarded it simply as a Romish device, covering some underhand injury to their faith, and at all events involving some submission to the Papal court which had promulgated the change. In Edenberg the calendar was preached against vehemently. This was construed into sedition, for which the city was heavily fined and deprived of several of its privileges. The pastors were banished, and stringent orders issued by the Archduke Ernest—the regent—that no preacher should be admitted into Edenberg unless with consent of the bishop, nor any religious ceremonies performed by any but regular Romish priests.

"As this letter was read in the magistrates' council, it cast the town into indescribable sorrow and consternation. Thousands should live without the comforts of the gospel, children should be unbaptized, the sick should die without the voice of a spiritual comforter, and the dead should be buried according to the rites of the Romish Church. Yet one thing remained. At the distance of about five English miles were two villages where the gospel was preached still, for these villages did not belong to Edenberg. Faith gave the citizens strength, and they streamed out to these villages to hear the word of God; and though many of them were taken prisoners and carried off to the bishop's residence, still the enemy did not succeed in destroying the Protestant Church in that city."

Even at the Diet, the Gregorian calendar was only adopted by the states "from respect to our king, but not as an acknowledgment of Roman supremacy."

Nine hundred Protestant congregations are reported to have existed in Hungary during the first years of the Emperor Rudolph, besides seventy among the Slavack population. Zwinglians were chiefly found in those provinces where the Turk gave them a toleration which even their own Lutheran brethren would not give. The approach of Mohammed the Third, with a hundred and fifty thousand Moslem soldiers, was looked upon as a blessing rather than a misfortune by this large minority of Hungarians. He would divert the force of their persecutors, and wherever fell the shadow of his standard was toleration. Waves of war swept over the country. Do we ever thank God for our peaceful churches, where we worship Sabbath after Sabbath, no man making us afraid? These Hungarian Protestants dare worship in no other fashion than harnessed for battle—the sword in one hand, the dearly-bought Bible in the other.

Monks yet show, at the richly-endowed convent of Radna, that picture of the Virgin which was flung into the fire by the infidels, but would not burn. Only a certain blackening with smoke is offered as proof of the miracle and reason why the daub—of a female encircled with a large gilt crown—should perform sundry other miracles, bringing large revenues to its owners. By its side is preserved a stone, to which the Virgin of the picture affixed the horse's hoofs of a scoffing Turk, who doubtless did not believe in the canvas idol.

Ten thousand Roman troops came to help Rudolph against the Turks. They were just as bitter enemies to the Protestant as to the Moslem. An imperial general named Basta desolated Transylvania, and made himself a proverb to succeeding generations by his cruelty to the Reformed population. The language of the country to this day embodies a characteristic trace of him. Travellers see a large wheelbarrow in ordinary use, and are told that these are "Basta szekér"—"Basta's carriages"—to which he harnessed men instead of beasts, and thus made them draw the forage and camp equipage of his army.

Basta's Carriages.

Far worse than this was done by his orders. More than once a pile of Protestant books was made the fuel for burning a Protestant pastor. Others of these unfortunate men were flayed alive, while gentle Mother Church stayed not the tyrant's hand, but aided and abetted through her episcopal agents. He seems, indeed, to have meditated a destruction after the pattern of the far-famed St. Bartholomew, for the Roman commander who acted in concert with him declared that their plan was to put to the sword every grown person in Hungary and Transylvania who should not become a Roman Catholic.

A fearful famine followed the ravages which these defenders of the faith committed, so fearful that the crowning crime and curse denounced in Deut. xxviii. 56, was fulfilled in a Christian country. "The tender and delicate woman" cast evil eyes upon the children she had borne and slew them secretly for food, owing to "the want of all things in the straitness" of the famine. A shocking cannibalism was practiced by the starving people. Even the bodies of the dead were not safe from outrage.

And where was the king of Hungary, who had solemnly sworn at his coronation to govern this nation with justice and mercy? Was he aware of the barbarities practiced by his generals in his name and the name of religion? Rudolph lived in the recesses of his palace at Prague, surrounded by artists, alchemists and astrologers, lapping himself in a life of slothful ease and debauchery. His existence was wasted in the veriest trifles, while no single duty of his high station was fulfilled. In permitting persecution of the Protestants he was obeying his ghostly advisers, who from childhood had trained him to be their tool. A German historian says of him that "for the gratification of his covetousness he transgressed all law and all morality in order to bury his treasures by the million." Consequently his unpaid troops forced subsistence and plunder from every land into which they came, and in Hungary they found it most profitable and least dangerous to pillage the Protestants.

CHAPTER XX.

THE FREE CITIES.

ALL over Europe these have proved the nurseries of liberty, both civil and religious. In Hungary they made a strong stand against the tyranny of the bishops, and only where main force was exercised to override their privileges did popery prevail.

Thus in Kashaw the bishops, bringing with them the Roman general Barbiano and his soldiers, succeeded in suppressing all outward signs of Protestantism. The pastors were banished, the church handed over to a priest, and lest the people should imitate those of Edenberg and go to neighbouring villages to hear the gospel, heavy fines were denounced as the penalty for doing so.

The five mining cities knew that this example was levelled at them, and determined to stand staunchly by their faith. Presently a demand came from the bishop of Raab—who also wielded civil force, as being deputy governor of Hungary

—that the magistrates of Lentshaw should give up to him all their churches, schools, hospitals, ministers' houses—in fact, every tittle of ecclesiastical property, to be used as he should think fit.

The burgomaster would give no precipitate answer to such a proposal. He summoned a meeting of the citizens for consultation, where every man might speak his mind on the momentous subject. According to the custom of the times—when early rising seems to have been easier than now—this meeting of the masses took place at seven in the morning. They heard the bishop's letter read, and then the principal pastor spoke to them. "He did give," state the town records, "a beautiful warning to hold fast by the word of God. He would risk his body, honour, property and life to abide with us. Upon which the judges and the town council, together with the citizens and their reverend ministers, did bind themselves with an oath to risk their liberty, honour, property and life for the word of God and the Augsburg Confession, and never to perjure themselves, so help them God and his holy word."

Such answer received the bishop of Raab to his demand. He came in person, but not having military force enough to crush the citizens, his attempt at despotism raised a tumult, whence he escaped by flight. Cajolings and threatenings alike failed. On one occasion the reply to his messenger, who had promised in his name many favours if the city would only yield, was so terse as this: "We will rather have God for our friend than the devil and all his followers."

CHAPTER XXI.

"THE TWENTY-SECOND ARTICLE."

THE laws passed by the Diet of Presburg in 1604 consisted of twenty-one articles or acts; yet when these were promulgated, Hungarians found that a twenty-second article had been added, to which no hereditary magnate or chosen deputy had affixed his assent. It contained matter quite opposed to the spirit of the Hungarian parliament, which had shown a strong disapprobation of religious persecution. It decreed that all the old laws against heresy—even that which prescribed burning alive as a form of cure—should be rigidly observed; it set forth as a royal duty the maintenance of the Romish superstition by every means, and the utter extirpation of Protestants.

And who had dared thus forge a decree which had never passed the Diet, and to add it to those which were genuine? Priests had persuaded King Rudolph to do so. The monarch, who never stirred out of his Prague palace—at one time he was so many months without appearing beyond its bounds that the citizens became convinced he was dead, and a formidable riot was only quelled by his showing himself at a window—did in his luxurious retreat among his artists, alchemists and astrologers, deliberately authorize a despotic decree, which, in violation of his oath to the Hungarian constitution, placed the liberties and lives of his worthiest subjects at complete disposal of the Romish clergy; and he did so simply because he was irritated by the presentation of two petitions from the Protestants in his dominions, humbly requesting that they might be allowed to live and to worship God as their consciences dictated.

The "twenty-second article" made it penal for them to remonstrate in future, no matter how severe the treatment they received. Like dumb animals, they must submit to the spoiler, and even die in silence.

All the free blood in Hungarian hearts was excited against this aggression. If the king were allowed to add what laws he pleased to those sanctioned by the Diet, their free constitution was not worth more than the parchment on which it was written: Rudolph would speedily become in practice what he was by nature—a thorough despot. The states protested against "the twenty-second article," and the prince-palatine, viceroy of Hungary, affixed his seal to the protest.

But the bishops and the generals had now what they wanted, a royal authorization for their persecution of Protestants, and cared very little that the states which they oppressed disapproved of the oppression.

CHAPTER XXII.

MATTHIAS BOTSKAY.

WHEN the sufferings of the children of Israel under heathen tyrants were at their worst, then would God raise up from their number some man to be a judge and a deliverer. Such a one was Matthias Botskay to the Hungarians at this time. A prince of the best blood, he had long since revolted against the barbarities inflicted on his fellow-countrymen by foreign soldiers. He had first made a journey to Prague for an audience of the lazy king, and been refused admittance with every mark of disrespect. Returning home with heart chafed and angered, he found that the Protestants under his protection and living on his estates had been cruelly treated by the Roman general Barbiano, who had also attacked and plundered two of Botskay's castles. He levied his vassals and marched after the invader. Barbiano was defeated and fled. "Give me shelter within your walls," he cried to the inhabitants of Kashaw, whom he had lately deprived of their pastors and churches, but they would not. "You are a destroyer of those who believe on God," they assigned as a reason; and the baffled persecutor had to flee farther, while they opened their gates to Botskay. And it was the prompt measures of the latter, ending in another victory, which prevented the accomplishment of Basta's bloody intention to slay every grown-up Protestant throughout Hungary.

The insurrection spread so widely among the outraged subjects of Rudolph that in a short space of time only a few border towns in Upper Hungary remained faithful to him. The free city of Edenberg was one of these, notwithstanding the injuries that had been inflicted on its inhabitants in his name. Botskay besieged it. The Austrian commander threatened to throw all the children into the fosse of the castle, if they and their mothers were not sent out of the town as useless mouths. Happily, a truce was concluded between the contending parties in time to prevent any measure so dreadful; and the bishop, taking advantage of the pause in conflict, seized all the church treasures in Edenberg, plate and money, and made his escape. Not very far, however: the burgomaster had warned him that the country was overrun with bands of plundering Turks: he and his train of clergy were pillaged at Steinanger, and barely saved their lives.

The Turks were in alliance with Botskay. Mohammed the Third sent him a crown, but the Protestant champion laid it aside, remarking that there was already a legally-crowned king of Hungary, whose rights he had no desire to invade. He wished simply to free his brethren from wrong, and would sheathe his sword when their liberties were guaranteed.

A certain evangelical nobleman, named Count Stephen Illyesházy, had been deprived of his estates and banished to Holland by the fanatical zeal of the Romish party. With deep sadness he viewed the rent and miserable condition of his native land, and offered his mediation, exile as he was, to conclude peace if possible. That alliance with the Turks had made Botskay of such consequence that King Rudolph (who was also emperor) was glad to receive the overture; and the exile's exertions ended in the Peace of Vienna, 1606.

CHAPTER XXIII.

THE PEACE OF VIENNA.

NOW was the notorious "twenty-second article" formally declared an illegal addition to the statutes of Hungary, no longer binding on any subject of the emperor. Further triumph had the Protestants in the abolition of all decrees that had been enacted against them. The treaty declared that every Hungarian should have perfect liberty of conscience, which even the king had no power to limit or disturb in any manner.

So far was wrung from Rudolph and his fanatical advisers, but a clause was added by which they hoped to nullify the force of the concession: "It was not to be interpreted in any way detrimental to the Roman Catholic religion." A great deal might be made of these few words in clever and unscrupulous hands, and undoubtedly they served their purpose of sowing discord in the very heart of peace.

Matthias Botskay would not for a long time accept of the clause, until the greatest persuasion had been used and the most solemn assurances been given by the archduke-regent that nothing damaging to Protestant interests was intended. The approaching Diet could settle all. At last the treaty was signed by the leading magnates of Hungary, and guaranteed by the states of Bohemia, Silesia and Moravia.

Other of its articles bear the stamp of the time and the occasion as regards religion. The Jesuits, who had behaved so badly in Transylvania that the Diet had declared their academy at Klausenberg to be a fortress erected against the liberties of the country, were prohibited from ever possessing landed or house property. "They had sent their fanatical students into the houses of Calvinists searching for books, which they brought out and burned; this illegal conduct often ended in bloodshed and pillage." King Rudolph reserved a right to make them presents, which was some salve to this wound. Two prelates, who had been particularly active against the Reformed party, were forbidden to return to Hungary till they should be legally purged of certain charges. Public offices and military appointments were to be open to all Hungarian subjects, without distinction of creed. Ecclesiastical abuses generally were referred to the forthcoming Diet.

Great was the joy among the oppressed Protestants at the full recognition of their claims, so stringently guaranteed. A cloud, small as a man's hand appeared on the horizon, in the shape of a protest from the pope. He would have none of the peace which was adverse to the interests of bigotry; sooner civil war and all its woes than that Bible-readers should go free. Sacerdotal cabals were set to work to nullify the Treaty of Vienna.

Botskay's death was the first calamity that befel the Reformed. Somebody poisoned him the year after the peace; his body-guards believed it to be done by the chancellor of Transylvania, and hewed him to pieces in the public streets accordingly. The murdered man was "a generous and noble prince," says the chronicler. Well he kept watch and ward over the liberties of his brethren of the faith; and the enemy knew that after his death they were in a manner defenceless. "Once more began the oppression—once more was it forbidden to the Protestants to bring their complaints before the Diet—once more were successful attempts made to deprive them of their churches"—though the Peace of Vienna had distinctly stipulated that each party should be left in tranquil possession of their own.

But truly the peace was no peace until its jesuitical clauses were removed and the unworthy Rudolph was dethroned. His brother, the archduke-regent, had summoned a Diet to confirm the treaty; and against the very first sentence, which guaranteed perfect liberty to Hungarian Protestants, the bishops and clergy entered a warm remonstrance. The king, upholding them, declared all the decisions of the Diet null and void; whereupon the country revolted and the archduke was offered the crown, on condition that he signed articles confirming the Protestant claims.

Afterward was calm for a while; and the Reformed churches had leisure to attend to their internal organization and set the house in order, now that it was no longer in a state of siege.

CHAPTER XXIV.

THE SYNOD OF SILLEIN.

THIS obscure village became famous in Hungarian ecclesiastical history for a gathering of clergy convened by the magnate and palatine, George Thurzo, with a view of arranging church government. They did so after the manner of a republic. A system of deacons, seniors, inspectors and superintendents was settled. Three circles, with as many superintendents, comprised the ten counties represented at the synod. All these officers of the Church were appointed by election. A particular duty of the superintendent in his yearly visits to a congregation was to inquire into the matter and the manner of its minister's preaching. Might not our modern churches take a hint here? For surely "the matter and the manner of preaching" includes much of a minister's efficiency, since it has pleased God by such "foolishness to save those who believe."

Eighteen days after the meeting of the synod, the worshippers at the Church of St. Martin, in Presburg, might have been seen to gather in groups about the principal door, reading some document which was fastened to it by a nail. And the faithful crossed themselves as they perceived how heavily weighted with curses was this publication of their cardinal-primate, wherein he called the Reformed clergy by no gentler name than wolves, denounced their impiety in daring to elect superintendents, and demanded that they should forthwith revoke all the acts of the synod as illegal.

The paper which the Reformed put forth as answer was headed with the suitable motto, "Stand fast therefore in the liberty wherewith Christ hath made us free, and be not entangled again in the yoke of bondage." They would give up no whit of their rights, and appealed to the king. The first nobleman in Hungary, the palatine or viceroy Thurzo, was warmly on their side. We find that to his wife was dedicated the Magyar translation of Luther's admirable Shorter Catechism, used in teaching Protestant children. The family name appears henceforth very frequently among the upholders of the truth, which proves that the noble lady taught her own children that religion which she patronized.

An opposition synod was held by the cardinal, in which the chief business—besides denouncing that of Sillein—was the prohibition of priests' marriage and of the cup at the sacrament. And the new king, Matthias, to whom the Protestants had appealed, disowned their right to appoint superintendents or to organize any ecclesiastical system.

A book written by a renegade, the Cardinal Pazmány, at this time did the Reformed cause much injury. He was born of a Protestant family, but in his youth joined the Jesuits, among whom he soon rose to eminence, and was specially intrusted with the Hungarian mission. His book was "The Guide to Truth," in which he whitewashed his chosen Church with remarkable ability and success, directing particular energy to that black spot on her practice which keeps no faith with heretics. Full of sophistry, and dressed in a style popular and attractive, the volume was widely read, and in consequence "many persons left the Reformed communion altogether; but the loss was to the Protestant Church only like the stucco falling from a building while the structure remained still secure." Nobody answered the book, though Count Esterházy wrote a dialogue exposing the errors of the Romish Church.

CHAPTER XXV.

THE SECOND FERDINAND.

KING MATTHIAS had no children, and the Papal party, who dreaded a really free popular election to the realm of Hungary, persuaded him to resign that crown in favour of their devoted ally, the Archduke Ferdinand of Austria. And so in 1618 a Diet was summoned at Presburg for the nominal choice of the new monarch.

Among the sixteen articles proposed in the Diet as conditions for the king, the sixth bound him "to grant a universal, unlimited, unrestrained liberty of public worship in every place and in every way, as had been guaranteed by the Peace of Vienna." After considerable squabbling, Ferdinand accepted of the terms, which went sorely against the grain of his character. He was one of the most bigoted and superstitious men alive, but he had just now to please the Protestants, and when he promised them full protection by this sixth stipulation, he added in lofty language that he would sooner lose his life than break his word.

The antecedents of his history might indeed have given cause for fear. Before the Virgin's image at Loretto he had made a vow "to banish all Protestants out of his estates, should it cost him his heart's blood," and he had knelt to receive the pope's blessing on the resolve. He was an enthusiast and a fanatic as to her worship. He believed that she had spoken to him—that he had heard her voice in words of comfort as he lay praying opposite a crucifix during a storm. She was his goddess; he named her generalissimo of all the forces of the Austrian empire, and he believed that it pleased her to persecute the Reformed.

How could he, then, have taken a solemn oath "to grant unlimited, unrestrained liberty of worship in every place?" The explanation, in his own royal words, is worth remembering as a specimen of jesuitical reserve: "With my mouth did I indeed swear to the Protestants, but with my heart to the Roman Catholics."

The renegade, Cardinal Pazmány, having all the bitter spirit of a renegade, injured his former coreligionists in every way he could, secure that the royal oath would oppose no obstacle. He was primate now, and influential in the Diet, and declared that "he would rather see his villages forsaken of all their inhabitants and lying waste than that on his estates a single church should exist for the benefit of Protestant subjects." Count Stephen Pallfy, a magnate, went the length of erecting a gallows on which to hang any Reformed ministers who should enter his territories without leave. This was hardly "unrestrained liberty of worship!"

In order to swamp the Protestant votes at the Diet, Ferdinand the Second created, in one year, twenty-two princes with sixty counts and barons. Such an overwhelming majority of court creatures enabled the promise-breaking king to do much as he chose with the religious liberties of his people.

"I would rather have a wasted than an accursed kingdom," was his remark when the evil tidings of rebellion and civil war reached his council-chamber; and history records that his bigotry contrived "to depopulate his monarchy of one million of human beings."

CHAPTER XXVI.

PRINCE BÉTHLÉN GÁBOR.

HE has been called the Cromwell of Transylvania, for his untiring energy and resolution in the cause of religious liberty. A prince by birth, he devoted his life to the oppressed Protestants of Hungary, not hesitating to oppose the imperial might of Ferdinand with the force of his small province. Again were the Turks good allies to the good cause, and by their help he conquered even the capital, Presburg, and got possession of the Hungarian crown of St. Stephen, the national palladium.

Then he stretched out his hand of help to the Bohemian Protestants, who were struggling for the commonest rights of toleration, the want of which would now rouse the sympathies of enlightened Europe. We have all heard of the Thirty Years' War, which made a desert of the fairest parts of Germany, owing to the bigotry of Ferdinand and his Jesuit advisers. Béthlén

Gábor was one of the earliest actors on the field. At the Diet of Nusohl, 1620, imperial commissioners were ready to guarantee what had been so often royally guaranteed and so often broken—the old arrangement for religious freedom in Hungary—but they would say nothing about Bohemia. Béthlén (this was his family surname; for we have seen how the Magyar language requires the baptismal name in the second place, and German historians accordingly call him Gabriel Béthlén) would not relinquish his suffering friends, even to his own advantage, but made a tighter treaty with them than ever. Ferdinand's representatives withdrew, and Count Emerich Thurzo, the chiefest Protestant magnate, who also was palatine, proposed and carried a resolution that Prince Béthlén should be proclaimed king of Hungary.

Like the Englishman whom he resembles, he refused the dignity. He was satisfied with his princedom of Transylvania, and his noblest ambition was to deliver his brethren in the faith from persecution. Personal aggrandizement would be set down as the motive of his movements if he accepted the crown; and he was a God-fearing man; piety was the prevailing current of his life. Some of his psalms are still sung in the Reformed churches; and Romish chroniclers record with wonder that he had read the Bible, from cover to cover, twenty times. Not all the entreaties of the Diet, nor the representations of his less wise Protestant friends and pastors, could prevail on him to step upon the glittering eminence of the throne. Four days after the offer he dissolved the Diet, having first confirmed its fifty-two laws, among which were several which bore on the state of religion in the country.

Perfect equality was decreed to the members of "the three confessions—Lutheran, Reformed or Zwinglian and Arian;" but "attacks on each other in writings and sermons were forbidden." The Synod of Sillein was confirmed. The Jesuits were banished; also the renegade Cardinal Pazmány as a "seditious man and an enemy of Hungary." Tithes and church dues were to fall to the clergy of all confessions alike; but three Romish bishops were declared sufficient for the needs of that persuasion in the country. "Such church property as had hitherto tended to encourage luxury among the clergy, and such as had been abused to the persecution of members of other confessions, and thus to disturbance of the peace, should be confiscated to the crown."

These laws were made with the assent of many distinguished Catholic magnates, who recognized the righteous claims of their Protestant fellow-subjects; but King Ferdinand would have none of them; and as to Bohemia, he went on persecuting there to his heart's content. Twelve thousand worthy Christians (among whom were one hundred and eighty-five nobles) were driven into exile in England, Flanders, Switzerland; which exile often meant starvation. Béthlén remonstrated, and backed his remonstrance in the only manner effectual with Ferdinand's priestly councillors—he crossed Hungary with a great army. Passing through Tyrnau, he endowed an evangelical school with a maintenance for twenty-four free scholars. Wherever he went freedom followed and true Christianity raised her head. George of Brandenburg came to help him with troops. Peace was made and broken several times. Never were the terms of the Treaty of Vienna observed, except at the edge of the sword. What sacred sanctions could be invoked to make those fulfil their compact whose priests enjoined no faith with heretics?

Béthlén's struggle against injustice was nearly ended, when the peace of Presburg added another to the broken guarantees of religious liberty. He died in the following year, 1629, and forthwith the oppressor began again to violate all promises.

Ferdinand the Second continued to act thus systematically until his own death in 1637. "Scarce can the eye find a single point in his reign of eighteen years on which to rest with satisfaction. In Germany his fanaticism had driven the religious war to the worst pitch. Magdeburg contained twenty-six thousand corpses of men, women and children who had perished by the hand of his general Tilly. Bohemia, Moravia and a great part of Hungary were miserably oppressed. What had he gained? A few stone churches and schools, stolen from the Lutherans and Calvinists; a hundred thousand converts brought over to Rome by sword, prison or bribery," and the perishing of one million of his subjects by war and famine. For all these benefits rendered to the popish cause the Cardinal Pazmány and Bishop Matthew of Reustadt asserted that Ferdinand passed immediately into heaven, without experiencing the pains of purgatory!

CHAPTER XXVII.

RAKOTZY'S REBELLION.

FOR years after the death of Béthlén Gabor the records of the Church in Hungary present one monotonous picture of suffering. Not violent persecution, but every annoyance that could be inflicted—wrong and robbery in particular—was the experience of the Protestants in the realms of Ferdinand the Third. Again they looked toward Transylvania for help, and Prince George Rakotzy raised the standard of revolt as their only earthly hope.

The king at once issued a proclamation full of beautiful promises, but few could be deceived by them now. Were not his generals—in safe and undisturbed countries—threatening to hang any worshippers in Protestant churches upon gallows erected before the doors? Moravian exiles who had lived peacefully in Skalitz for twenty years were banished on the world as paupers. But rapid justice followed this piece of tyranny. Count

Robert Douglas, a Scottish captain under Rakotzy, hastened to that city and reinstated them.

From the far frozen North did aid also come. Rakotzy made alliance with Protestant Sweden as well as with Mohammedan Turkey. The best soldier against him was Prince Esterházy, who had once professed the faith which now he sought to destroy. On certain estates of his, where the people were nearly all Protestants, he took possession of their churches, schools, ministers' houses, and banished the pastors and schoolmasters. And still he found few to follow his own faithless example for either gain or dread.

France offered to aid Rakotzy with money—not that her most Christian king cared for the patriots' cause, but that he wished to damage the House of Hapsburg and weaken Austria. These alliances made the prince of Transylvania so formidable that a very favourable peace was concluded at Linz, which has been called "the second pillar of the rights of the Protestant Church in Hungary." Ninety churches were to be restored, but then three hundred had been lost. The Reformed might build new ones, with the probable chance that they were building them in reality for the papal party. A needful and far-sighted paragraph was inserted that "at every Diet his majesty should inquire into the complaints of the Protestants and have them redressed." So certain was it that there must be causes of complaint!

This first Rakotzy died in 1648, but his son and successor was just as staunch a Reformer as himself. When the Jesuits worked their way into the country again, in spite of the laws for keeping them out, he quietly got a list made of them and their disguises, and suddenly required them all to remove beyond the frontier.

CHAPTER XVIIII.

THE PALATINE AND THE ARCHBISHOP.

THE greatest layman in Hungary was the palatine or viceroy. Chosen by the king as his representative, he was nevertheless elected also by the Diet. Generally the names of two Catholic and two Protestant magnates were proposed by the king, among which lay the Diet's right of choice.

The greatest churchman in Hungary was the primate-archbishop of Grán. Vast was the influence of this line of prelates. They had the right of conferring a sort of nobility, which was hereditary. Their revenues were little below those of royalty. They wielded the pope's power with local knowledge of how to apply it. The present wearer of this mitre was George Lippay, a very earnest persecutor. Wherever he had sufficient authority he banished the Reformed pastors and placed Jesuits in their stead, in spite of the wishes of the people or the statute-book of the land. So bitterly did he oppose everything like toleration at the Diet which confirmed the peace of Linz that he had to be threatened with the deprivation of his lay offices by the wiser statesmen about the king.

Sometimes these chief powers, lay and clerical, had a collision, especially if the palatine happened to be a liberal-minded man. Count Paul Pallfy, a Catholic Hungarian of the highest rank, held the office at a Presburg Diet, 1649. The Magnate Chamber was assembled, presided over by the palatine. The archbishop was not in his place, and the whisper went that he was paying a morning visit to the king. As religious matters were to be discussed, the magnates waited for him deferentially, until at last, when much time had elapsed, the palatine rose to open the subject by saying that the king had assured him it was his earnest desire that all quarrels about religion should be amicably arranged; but when the archbishop entered, without having heard what had gone before, he rose to assure the assembly that the king had just said to him the very opposite.

Which was true? After a pause of astonishment at the conflicting statements, a magnate suggested that a mixed deputation should wait on his majesty, consisting of an equal number of Catholic and Protestant nobles, to ascertain what he really had said. They returned with a confirmation of the palatine's words, whereupon he turned indignantly to the archbishop and demanded how he had dared thus to misrepresent the king and disturb the peace of the Diet? "If it were not for your cloth, Sir Churchman, I should know how to treat you as you deserve!"

But Lippay had spoken in the same spirit as that of a declaration he had made shortly before, that the king could tolerate Protestants only as thieves and robbers are borne with—just so long as it is impossible to eradicate them. And his great power as prince-primate—"beyond all example," says one writer*—enabled him to be a very effectual oppressor. One of his last actions was to eject all the Protestants from a certain village and fill their place with Roman Catholics.

The king, Ferdinand the Third, tried hard to be a just man. He had chosen for his motto, "The fear of God and justice." He desired to hold the balance evenly between contending parties, and was able to succeed so far as that his Protestant subjects had a little breathing-time toward the close of his life.

* Grán is still the richest see in Europe.

CHAPTER XXIX.

THE JESUITS' GOLDEN AGE.

THIS reign, which lasted half a century (1657–1705) has been called "the golden age of the Jesuits," whence may be gathered how injurious it was to Protestantism. The young emperor had been educated for a priest, and his blind adherence to Rome through all his days proved that he would have made a useful ecclesiastic.

The first Diet opened with fair promises, because the grand vizier of Turkey was approaching with great force; his second Diet (the danger over) opened with a memorial from the Protestant deputies, containing the bitterest charges against "those who have by violence, for many years, habitually transgressed the laws of the land and prevented the exercise of that toleration secured by statute." Forty churches had been forcibly taken away from their Protestant builders and owners during the last three years. A sort of dragonnade had taken place in some parishes, and soldiers been billeted on the people till they became Romanists. Count Nadásdy sent an armed force to one church, had the bells rung as if for worship, and when the congregation assembled the doors were shut, mass celebrated, and a priest administered the wafer all round in spite of every resistance; which act made them all Roman Catholics, according to papal law. In another parish, the same count ordered that the Protestants passing through one of his forests to church, should be stripped of their clothes and sent home naked. Another nobleman made up a list of the Protestants on his estates, and gave each an intimation that if he did not become a Catholic he should be banished, retaining of all his worldly goods only four florins for the journey. On such as were not influenced by this threat he billeted his Wallack soldiery—"the European Indians;" and the few who withstood both arguments he convinced by imprisonment in his castle dungeons. Those who have visited Hungarian dungeons are not surprised to hear that this method of conversion too often proved effectual.

Hundreds of such stories could be told. But the repetition of such facts would be wearisome. A general crushing of the Reformed faith went on throughout Hungary, in spite of the written and sworn laws. We read of one nobleman who caused a great fire to be kindled in the hall of his castle, and threw therein all the books of the Protestant pastor. The holy Bible itself was fixed on a spit and turned round in a process of gradual singeing and roasting, while the count and his friends stood by enjoying the spectacle. By some sudden blast several leaves of the Bible were blown about, and one was driven directly toward the count's breast. Baron Ladislaus Revay caught at it, but it was seized out of his hand by the count, who began to read. It happened to be a portion of the fortieth chapter of Isaiah, and the first words he read were, "The grass withereth, the flowers fadeth, but the word of our God shall stand for ever."

This Jehoiakim conduct had a like punishment. The count was afterward mixed up in some treason which caused his death on the scaffold, and when he stepped upon it to meet the headsman's sword, he said, "The Lord is just in all his ways!" and his burial was that of a malefactor.

Those magnates who were less severe against their heretic serfs were threatened with punishment by the bishops. All over the country pastors were lingering in prison, for no other offence than doing as the law authorized them—preaching the gospel to their own Protestant people. Scores of acts of oppression were established by overwhelming evidence in their memorial to the emperor-king, Leopold, and in five subsequent memorials, delivered at intervals; but his answer (after long delays) was that the Protestant deputies "should not annoy his majesty with such complaints at the Diet, when something more important had to be done. For all these religious grievances the law had already made full provision."

An equivocation worthy of a Jesuit's pupil! Truly the law was well enough, but never were its enactments carried out. It was mockery to point for redress to statutes which were systematically disregarded by persons in power. So thought the Romanist palatine Vesselényi, as he handed the king's sealed answer to "the faithful members of the Evangelical Confessions assembled at the Diet," according to superscription. "I had rather the funeral bell tolled over me than live to see this day," were the high-spirited magnate's words to them. "May this hour be covered with eternal darkness!"

After another fruitless appeal for justice, asking

it "for the sake of the mercy of God, and for the sake of the blood of Jesus shed on the cross," the Reformed deputies came to the resolution of leaving the Diet, where their most important affairs were treated with scorn; and no persuasion could induce them to return.

Then began a long struggle with the court, ending in ruin to the Reformed party. The sword has seldom been God's weapon to ensure the victory of his cause. Multitudes were banished or put to death. One incident we select from the painful catalogue.

Nicholas Drabik was a Moravian by birth and by religion, and had fled to Hungary from the persecutions in his own country carried on by the same rulers of the house of Hapsburg. An humble and poor man, whose livelihood was "dealing in a small way in woollen wares," already he was eighty-four years old, and might have seemed scarce worthy prey for the ecclesiastical courts. But he had written a little book of prophecies, named "Light out of Darkness," in which he called King Leopold and his predecessors covenant-breakers, and compared the house of Austria to the house of Ahab—unpleasant and uncourtly truths. So he was brought on a cart to Presburg for trial, and sat on the ground before his judges, because from the weakness of age he could not stand.

When his belief was inquired for, he repeated the whole Athanasian Creed. "I believe all that," said the archbishop, "but also a great deal more which is necessary." The old man rejoined, sharply (having not the reposeful manners of high life, but being, in truth, in desperate circumstances), "You don't believe any such thing. You believe in your riches and estates."

He acknowledged the authorship of the little book, which, indeed, had not done much harm in Hungary, as it was composed in Bohemian, the only language known to the old peddler. Death was the sentence pronounced upon him; and such death! First his right hand was to be amputated; his tongue to be cut out and nailed to a post; his head to be cut off; his body burned in the market-place, together with his writings.

Remanded to prison till all this could be suitably done, the Jesuit fathers came to him. "Your life if you recant," said they, as the old man brooded over his fate, "and we will send you back to your own country, Moravia, there to die in peace."

Was it any wonder that he yielded? He said

that he would become a Romanist for his life's sake. Those of us who feel free from such weakness may cast the first stone at the aged prisoner. But the promise was all a lie; and, like our own Cranmer, the old man at execution declared that he would die in the faith which had sustained his life, and which he had only for a moment forsaken. To the letter was his sentence fulfilled.

The persecutions of the Church by Leopold would fill a volume. In the capital, Presburg, because the Protestant citizens refused to give up their churches and schools to the Romish clergy, they were declared guilty of treason, and their lives and property confiscated wholesale. After that sweeping sentence there was little difficulty in breaking open the doors, painting red crosses on the pillars and celebrating mass. The intercession of the elector of Saxony prevented any further violence, except that the ministers were shut up in prison, and finally banished.

This was in 1673. The same year an attempt was made on a grand scale to deprive the Protestant Church of its principal pastors, as knowing that sheep without a shepherd are easily misled. The archbishop of Grán, a distinguished persecutor, who had been going through his diocese with a retinue of Jesuits and dragoons, converting Protestants everywhere by a short and simple process, summoned thirty-three pastors from Lower Hungary to appear before the viceregal court at Presburg. Four prelates and some most bigoted magnates were to be their judges.

CHAPTER XXX.

TRIAL OF THE PASTORS.

VERY strange were some of the charges made against these thirty-three representative pastors. Not only were they accused of rebellion, correspondence with the Turks (who were indeed, far more friendly to them than so-called Christian powers), but of having stolen consecrated vessels and made banners of priests' vestments; of having called the Catholics worshippers of false gods; of having given the consecrated host to infidels. A long indictment, containing such articles, was read to the accused, but they were refused a copy of it. Mutual consultation for the purposes of defence was not allowed; and when once the superintendent was about to say something to exonerate himself, "Mr. Kalinka," said the archbishop of Grán, "there is no leave to speak here."

The thirty-three seemed to have been called together merely to be accused and sentenced. By their advocate they offered to clear themselves by oath from the more serious charges. At the close of the court the archbishop addressed to them a few superfluous sentences about his own merciful disposition. "My friends," said he, "I find no pleasure in killing, for I love peace. I could not look even on the death of a fowl. But I sit here as judge, and am compelled to obey the king's commands. Nevertheless, I shall do all I can for you." This was no obscure hint of the treatment they were to expect.

Next day, as they awaited their sentence, Count George Illyesházy came to them privately. "I sympathize deeply with you my poor friends," he began, "for you are to have a terrible sentence. Four of you will be put to the torture, have your hands struck off, and then suffer beheading. All the rest are to be exiled. I advise you to apply to the king for mercy. Cast yourselves on his gracious consideration." He also offered to act as mediator. Once he had been a Lutheran himself, and he understood their case.

"We are guiltless," said the pastors, "but we will obey our king in everything save matters of conscience."

Count George withdrew, and presently returned

with the names of those who were respectively to be tortured, beheaded and banished. They made the appeal for mercy which he advised. Banishment from home and country was the highest favour which these Protestant preachers could expect. What though their position had been established by the laws of Hungary as distinctly as the privileges of the nobles? These priestly despots cared not for the statute-book so long as they had the sword.

Finally an arrangement was made by which the lives of all these guiltless men were graciously spared, on condition that they signed a document stating that, "having been found guilty of rebellion, they, of their own free will, went into exile;" and it certainly was a fact that their free will chose banishment rather than torture and beheading. Some were allowed to stay in Hungary under safe-conducts, provided they also signed a declaration that, "having abused their office, they would, in future, abstain from every ministerial act." They were to live as private persons, if they had any way of earning their bread.

But dearer to the archbishop's heart, and more damaging to the Protestant cause than the crushing of the thirty, would have been the gaining two or three proselytes. He spoke privately to them, promising money and promotion to any who would join his Church. The royal treasury should be the bankers of such; they should have happy and prosperous lives, so far as filthy lucre can secure happiness. One man was found among the thirty to accept the degrading propositions; and from his surname, "Suhajda," was quickly formed by Hungarian wit the scathing anagram, "Ah, Judas!"

CHAPTER XXXI.

PASTORS TO THE GALLEYS.

THIS banishment of thirty-three pastors was merely an instalment of the work. The archbishop's next citation summoned three hundred and seven of them to appear before the same court at Presburg. Again did the Turks prove protectors, for the pasha-governor of countries on the frontier would not allow the ministers near him to attend.

Two letters, alleged to have been written by a deceased pastor, formed the foundation of a charge of rebellion against this multitude of ministers. Pretext for getting rid of them was all their enemies wanted; and when, after a month of "superficial investigation and debating, before men who were at the same time accusers, witnesses and judges," sentence of "beheading, confiscation, infamy, outlawry," was pronounced on the mass, "no one pretended that it had even the slightest appearance of justice. The design was to annihilate heretics, and fanaticism considered every means allowable."

Two hundred and thirty-six signed their resignation of the ministerial office and their own sentence of perpetual banishment, with the headsman's sword before their eyes. The rest held out. Five were chained together and thrown into a dungeon as encouragement to their brethren. Then twenty were brought in common country carts to Eberhard, the archbishop's palace-castle, and thrust into dark and filthy cells. Eighteen were sent to Leopoldstadt, having the hangman in the wagon for companion, who illustrated his religious zeal by beating their heads with his stick because they were heretics. A new amusement was also found for the archiepiscopal dessert. After dinner the prelate was wont to send for Protestant pastors from the dark and filthy cells aforesaid, and "after the bitterest insults and mockery, he sometimes descended to personal violence because they still steadily refused to sign the deed of demission. On one occasion he struck Stephen Nemethy with a hammer so violently that his arm was rendered almost useless."

When these were the actions of the head of the Hungarian hierarchy, what could be expected from its inferior members? The pressure of slow suffering began to produce the effect calculated on. Seventeen Lutherans renounced their faith at Komorn, and received each fifty florins reward, with liberty. And so elsewhere. But at Leopoldstadt, where the sufferers were staunchest, the Jesuit Kellio made them endure most. Coarse bread and water was their food. Each bore heavy chains day and night. They worked in these—dug away ice and snow and cleaned the sewers of the fortress. And some of the most honoured men in Hungary were thus treated. No assistance of money or food might be given them. A compassionate woman discovered in the act was put in a movable pillory and driven about the streets. One pastor, who refused to kneel as the consecrated wafer was carried by, was beaten till he bled. Two others, who were being taken by force to hear mass, tried to turn back at the church door, on which the enraged Kellio caused them to be stretched on the ground and belaboured with the ramrods of the soldiers' guns in such a manner that they died soon after.

Thirty-six pastors were taken from the fortress of Komorn on 11th March, 1675, and committed to a guard of cavalry for conveyance to Italy. They had been told that King Leopold was graciously pleased to spare their lives, "that they might learn to pray in the galleys." Chained in pairs, "under the mockery of the soldiers, they travelled on foot from Vienna to Trieste. Here the buttons were cut off their coats, their beards and heads shaved quite close so that they could distinguish each other only by the voice." Many died on the way, at which we do not wonder when we read that their daily provision was a quarter of a pound of biscuit and a glass of water, to which was sometimes added a bit of cheese. But further than Trieste was their journey, for the galleys lay at Naples, and they had to traverse so much of the peninsula wearily on foot. One exhausted man who fell on the road was left there unburied. Thirty were sold in Naples for fifty Spanish piastres each, and chained to the benches among thieves and murderers, their only crime preaching the truth of God's holy word.

CHAPTER XXXII.

DELIVERANCE BY THE DUTCH.

A KIND Christian lived in Naples, by name George Weltz, and God put it into his heart to visit these poor Hungarian slaves and relieve their numerous wants. He was wise in his generation, and paved his way by making presents to the inspector and being complaisant to the general in charge, so that at last this officer promised to set them free for the price of one hundred ducats apiece.

The gleam of hope was delusive; much more had to be done. Princes and peoples had interceded for them in vain. The elector of Saxony's spirited remonstrance with Leopold fell flat. Even our good-for-nothing Charles the Second issued a royal letter to the principal cities, the universities and prelates of England, desiring that a collection should be made for the release of these sufferers. The English ambassador at Naples supported George Weltz in his application to the Spanish regent Alvarez, wherein he stated that not for rebellion, but for their religion's sake alone, were these good men condemned to the most horrible slavery. Again Weltz offered to buy their freedom. "They are not Catholics," replied the regent, and because of this they could not even be ransomed.

But one day a Dutch squadron sailed into the Bay of Naples and took the case into its charge. The regent's scruples melted away, for De Ruyter was cruising not far off, and his name was a name of terror to oppressors. Presently he sailed into the harbour himself, and whereas to the commodore release of the prisoners had been promised within a given time, to the admiral, backed by all the power of the States-General, release was actually granted. The Neapolitan Supreme Court, under stimulus of his presence, declared "that the pastors and professors confined on board the galleys are not guilty of the charges laid against them, and shall without delay be set free."

The chaplain and principal officers of the Dutch fleet brought them the joyful news, and straightway the twenty-six Hungarian pastors—for to this number were they now reduced—were unchained amid tears of gladness, and with one acclamation they broke forth into the triumphant words of the hundred and twenty-fifth Psalm:

"They that trust in the Lord shall be even as Mount Zion,
Which cannot be removed, but abideth for ever!
As the mountains are round about Jerusalem,
So the Lord is round about his people from henceforth, even for ever."

And again:

"God is our refuge and strength, a very present help in trouble . . . .
Come, behold the works of the Lord . . . .
He maketh wars to cease unto the end of the earth:
He breaketh the bow and cutteth the spear in sunder: He burneth the chariot in the fire.
Be still, and know that I am God:
I will be exalted among the heathen."

Thus singing, in voices broken with emotion, they were brought over the waters of the beautiful bay to the ships of the commodore who had first made efforts for their deliverance. "He received and embraced them with unspeakable joy." Down upon the deck of the war-ship they all kneeled together, again to thank God even with weeping; and then arising, their full hearts found further utterance in singing another psalm!

"I love the Lord, because he hath heard my voice and my supplications.

Because he hath inclined his ear unto me, therefore will I call upon him as long as I live.

The sorrows of death compassed me, the pains of hell got hold upon me:

I found trouble and sorrow.

Then called I upon the name of the Lord: O Lord, I beseech thee, deliver my soul."

Next morning they were brought before the venerable De Ruyter himself. "It has given me more joy than all my victories," said this conqueror, "to have delivered you, the servants of Christ, from your intolerable slavery." When they would have essayed to thank him, "Give all the glory to God," he interposed; "I am only his instrument." And so the Dutch fleet sailed away from the bay of Naples, bearing with it these persecuted men, who finally found refuge in Holland and England.

CHAPTER XXXIII.

"IN DENS AND CAVES OF THE EARTH."

THE mountains have often been nurseries of God's truth and refuge for his servants, as were the Carpathians now. So effectually had the bigoted Leopold and his priests purged Hungary of heresy that, except in a few free cities or under the protection of one or two powerful magnates, his Protestant subjects dared not openly worship God. Unrepealed in the statute-book lay the laws of the land guaranteeing them equality of rights with their Catholic neighbours, but every day they were cast into prison, robbed and banished, for no other reason than that the strong hand of injustice was in the place of power.

Out in the heaths of Hungary, peopled with wild cattle and earless marmots—those vast steppes or "pusztas" that stretch five thousand square miles from Pesth to Transylvania—in lonely glens of the hills and glades of the forests, in ruined castles and deep morasses, among the frogs and leeches, lived the hunted Protestant pastors, having no certain dwelling-place. "From the dark cavern, scantily lighted, arose the psalm of praise to those wild melodies which to this day thrill the heart of the worshipper. From lips pale and trembling with disease, arising from a life spent in constant fear and danger, the consolations of the gospel were proclaimed."

Every effort was used by the enemy to discover such secret meeting-places. So base an action was committed as that a Jesuit assumed the garb of a pastor, borrowed his forms of speech, counterfeited his habits, and went about among the unsuspecting people to find out the secrets of their faith and the manner in which it was kept alive amid the storms of persecution. Betrayal followed; the peasant found that his guest had been a spy and informer.

In some places the smouldering fire broke out into actual rebellion. It is a meekness not to be expected in human nature that men can be plundered of all they hold dear in life and never raise an arm of resistance. Count Emerich Tokely, an ardent youth of twenty, gathered the insurgents into a force of many thousand men and carried on a guerrilla warfare for years. He said he would gladly lay down his arms as soon as Protestant rights were re-established. At last, because he was too successful, an armistice was concluded, pending the holding of a Diet in Edenberg.

There the Protestant States of Hungary approached their monarch with a memorial which ought to have covered his royal cheek with the crimson of shame. They complained of systematic and unceasing oppression, in spite of numberless laws to which his majesty had solemnly sworn. They had such cruelties to tell as that "some pastors have been stretched on the ground and nailed to wood in the form of a cross; others have been bastinadoed. After three attempts to hang a certain minister, he was at last buried alive! Even noblemen have been led in chains to attend on the Romish service. When psalms are sung or prayers offered in private houses the parties have been marched to prison as felons. Our brethren are not permitted to learn or practise a trade till they have renounced their faith." These were a few of the grievances endured by a large section of the Hungarian people. Four memorials to the king, and one to the queen, declaring such crying evils, remained unanswered. Until the deputies of thirteen Catholic counties joined in their prayer it obtained no heed.

Leopold then sent a message declaring that "all states in the whole land—magnates, nobles, free cities and royal boroughs—should remain by their religion. Not only should there be full liberty of faith, but also full and complete liberty of religious exercise in every form."

This seemed very fair, but the king had neither signed it nor sealed it with the imperial seal. Some days of further contest followed before this reasonable security could be obtained, and nothing was said of restitution. What about the nine hundred churches and school-houses that had been forcibly taken possession of by the Catholics?

One scarcely wonders to find such an aphorism as this current among the Protestant masses of Hungary: "Ne hidj neki mest Papista"—Don't believe him, he is a Papist." It was the popular translation of that "Punic faith" which so often sported with their hopes only to deceive them.

Things went on just as usual after the Diet. Pastors were hunted and people oppressed, as if there were no such thing as an imperial promise ever uttered.

CHAPTER XXXIV.

KARAFFA AND HIS BLUTSGERICHT.

HUNGARIAN Protestants lost a very important bulwark of protection when Buda was taken from the Turks in 1685. They had held it for a hundred and forty-six years, and all shades of faith were tolerated under the Crescent.

Leopold's general in Upper Hungary was Anton Karaffa, a name that has become famous for tyrannic cruelty. Nearly all the nobles of his district were Protestants, and he laid a plan for their ruin that amounted to a universal prescription. He accused them of rebellious tendencies en masse, and demanded full powers from Vienna to act as he thought proper.

"To punish the guilty according to the laws of Hungary," was the license given. It was scarcely probable that the assigned limit would be regarded by a savage soldier, who had declared that if a single nerve in his body was inclined to favour the Hungarians, he would cut it out and cast it on the fire. Karaffa forthwith established that court of judicature which quickly acquired the title of "Blood Council." Spies of the lowest grade rapidly filled his prisons with innocent victims. Thirty hangmen were in constant pay. Six hundred florins were paid for the invention of new tortures and modes of death. Perhaps it was then that an anguish was invented which has not been practiced in any other land but Hungary—the upper and lower jaws of a prisoner fastened together by a padlock passed through flesh and bone, and he left to die in a dark dungeon. The skeletons of such victims have been found even in our own day, mute victims of a fiendish barbarity.

Among ordinary executions, Sigismund Zimmerman, a distinguished senator and inspector of the evangelical Church, was beheaded after four hours on the wheel. Do we, comfortable Protestants of the nineteenth century, know what is meant by those awfully significant words—"on the wheel?" They mean that the principal bones in the body are broken, one after the other, by violent blows from a heavy iron bar. Other men were brought to the scaffold half-roasted by previous exposure to the fire. A son, whose father had been just executed, ascended it singing:

> "Lord Jesus Christ, my only light,
> The rock on which I build."

He was a young man of thirty years old, with wife and children to make life sweet to him.

All this went on without hindrance for months, and then a certain nobleman from Neusold, being put to the torture till he was nearly dead, was ransomed by a friend for ten thousand dollars. After a long nursing he recovered, and going to the Diet at Presburg, told his acquaintances what he had suffered. "Human nature could not bear so much," they said; whereupon he took them aside and showed them the scars on his limbs. This proof might not be gainsaid. Two of the deputies went to Vienna, and demanded of the emperor that Karaffa should be recalled and the "Blood Council" dissolved. The palatine Esterházy added his influence, and their request was granted, but Karaffa was received at court with all honour, and granted a medal as a mark of imperial approbation.

In the same Diet, Leopold proclaimed that his Protestant subjects had, by their dissatisfaction with their condition, forfeited all their privileges; nevertheless he would, of his royal favour, continue to them the liberties granted in 1681. It was not pleasant to hear—in the very year when William of Orange was freeing England from James the Second's tyranny—that the lives and property of the Protestant community in Hungary had no securer shelter than the favour of a bigot.

CHAPTER XXXV.

ANOTHER RÁKOTZY.

LEOPOLD'S promise of toleration gave little security. A royal commission for the settlement of religious affairs made matters worse than before. In Trentschin respectable citizens were publicly flogged on market-days for no other crime than that of being Protestants. They were compelled to attend all the processions, carrying flags or tapers. At Güns the Romish abbot aided the commissioner and put the pastor in chains. When a burger inquired on whose authority it was done, this military ecclesiastic pulled out a pistol and showed it as sufficient answer.

The land longed for a deliverer. The palatine-prince Esterházy received from Rome a dispensation permitting him to marry his brother's daughter, on the express condition that he should use his utmost endeavours to root out heresy. He faithfully fulfilled the compact, compelling whole villages on his estates to become Romanist. Numerous families were banished from house and home, sent forth as paupers on the wide world, because they would not comply. He commanded, under his seal as viceroy of Hungary, that all lieutenants of counties should be diligent to extirpate "these vermin." So efficacious were these measures that the Jesuits boasted they had gained eighteen thousand Hungarian converts in one year, and that the number of churches taken from the Protestants was past counting.

Rákotzy, prince of Transylvania, would not join these oppressors. On some pretext he was cast into prison, and would have been beheaded only for the immense bribe paid by his wife to the guards, who allowed him to escape to Poland. There he brooded over the wrongs of his country, and finally drew the sword in 1703. At first he was eminently successful. His armies swarmed round the very walls of Vienna. Half Hungary owned him as master. All the traditions of his race combined to urge him forward in his path of liberator. He could not be blinded by the old faithless promises. "Who can believe," he wrote to a mediating bishop, "that the court of Vienna intends to keep its word, when the Turks are invited to assist in crushing the Protestants, and the Jews promised a great reward for assassinating myself? The king acknowledges that the laws of the land have been transgressed by his officers, yet he does nothing to cause their injustice to cease. He refers only to some future Diet; but after what we have seen we may rather expect injustice to increase with the meeting of a Diet." Rákotzy refused to enter into any treaty the righteous performance of which should not be guaranteed by foreign powers.

The English ambassador, George Stepney, came forward to aid his fellow-Protestants in procuring favourable terms. Charles the Twelfth of Sweden did likewise. He also rendered material help to the Hungarian Church by ordering that four of his divinity students should be maintained at his expense in a German university. He gave twenty thousand dollars to an evangelical school, whose funds had been appropriated by the Jesuits.

It was unfortunate that Rákotzy's movement assumed a revolutionary aspect after the Diet of Onod, at which the Hungarian throne was declared vacant and the malcontent nobles attempted to set up a republic. Also the four creeds, Catholic, Lutheran, Calvinistic and Unitarian, were announced to have equal rights and privileges. One body only would not be tolerated: the Jesuits must be expelled. In a lengthened speech, Rákotzy recapitulated their evil deeds, their double-dealing: "Persecutions, confusions, endless mischief had they caused in all lands, especially in Hungary."

Though he was a Roman Catholic prince, the pope (Clement the Eleventh) excommunicated him for espousing the cause of heretics. Thenceforth his supporters began to fall off. The emperor Joseph gave some concessions which tempted away Protestants. That celebrated convention known as the Peace of Száthmar was concluded in 1711; it was guaranteed by England through the earl of Sutherland, and by Holland through Baron Rechtan. A few words from a state paper which these ambassadors presented to the emperor are worth quoting as illustrative of the oppression against which Rákotzy revolted and struggled for nine years:

"The conduct of the (Hungarian) landed proprietors in compelling those resident on their estates to adopt the landowners' religion, differs in no way from the awful French persecutions. The souls of men cannot be brought nearer to God by such treatment. If dragoons and hussars are proper persons to do the work of apostles of Jesus Christ, he would never have said, 'Behold, I send you forth as sheep among wolves.'"

The central stipulation of this Peace of Száthmar was, "perfect freedom to the Protestants." But the time was not yet.

CHAPTER XXXVI.

THE PESTH COMMISSION AND PRAGMATIC SANCTION.

CHARLES THE SIXTH, successor of Joseph (who died while the Peace of Száthmar was in the hands of plenipotentiaries) was the archduke for whom England had fought so strenuously that he might be set on the throne of Spain in opposition to the grandson of Louis the Fourteenth. "One of his first royal acts was to surrender the ancient crown of Hungary to deputies of the Hungarian nation;" it had long been shut up in the treasury at Vienna, and its absence from native soil was regarded with a perpetual discontent.

This conciliatory spirit was shown through the early part of his reign. He published so many petty decrees in favour of his Protestant subjects that the inference is irresistible that they were continually being oppressed by the bishops and other Romish powers. In one of these he commands that Protestant tradesmen shall not be punished for absenting themselves from the Catholic processions on Corpus Christi Day. Because he expressed his "royal will and pleasure" on such matters, it was argued by their enemies that Protestants had no legal rights, but were dependent on the passing caprice of the monarch. A new oath was invented to exclude all but Romanists from any office, containing the formula—"I swear by the Holy Virgin and all the saints;" and this was the cause of innumerable quarrels and heart-burnings, for no Protestant could take it.

The territory over which the Turks had ruled was the scene of hottest persecution now; for the Jesuits discovered a quibble which put the lives and property of the heretics there into their tender hands; this notable device was, that all edicts of toleration had been meant for that part of Hungary under Austrian sway, and therefore the newly-acquired countries had no claim whatever to freedom of conscience. And they acted accordingly.

Charles summoned a number of commissioners to meet at Pesth, and investigate the complaints which poured in from his Protestant subjects. They showed their bias at once by taking as the ground of their transactions a decree of 1707, in which it was declared that religious toleration must cease in those towns formerly on the borders, because they were now integral parts of the kingdom, and that in the newly-conquered territories no person must profess any religion but the Romish. The Evangelical Confessions protested; they demanded as the very first and most essential rule for the guidance of the commissioners, that they should "recognize religious liberty as the right of every one, in every station throughout the land of Hungary." So far from this point being yielded, even the Protestant commissioners themselves were forbidden by the Catholic majority to hold any public worship in Pesth. Finally the king was obliged to adjourn the commission in despair of its members doing anything but fight.

Not till 1730 was the result of its labours, and its folio volumes filled with conflicting evidence, made known to the empire in what are called "The Resolutions of Charles." They were drawn up by a council headed by the famous Prince Eugene of Savoy, and set forth that public worship could be permitted to Protestants only in the towns mentioned in a decree of Leopold's published fifty years before; that in other places family worship might be tolerated, provided only the members of each family were present, and such must employ the Romish priest for all baptisms, marriages and burials. All apostates shall be severely punished at the pleasure of the civil magistrate after due report to the king. Catholic holidays were to be observed by all Protestants, who were also to take part in every procession for the honour of the Virgin and saints, and must whenever required swear according to the "decretal oath," with the express clause, "By the Mother of God and all the Saints." In fact, all the injustice practised of late years was legalized.

After this came an imperial decree ordering that all churches in possession of Protestants, which had not been secured to them by express enactment, should be immediately confiscated. Says the chronicler: "It was midwinter, and a Hungarian winter!" when the Danube is blocked shore to shore with masses of ice, like the St. Lawrence, and forty degrees below the freezing point is nothing rare; "one may picture the distress of the people, but much more of the clergy and their families, who were all turned out on the world."

In Lower Hungary all this oppression was not

patiently borne. The whole congregation of a church sometimes consisted of the lesser orders of noblemen, who by the Golden Bull had many rights and privileges, and also had a mind to maintain them. Sometimes they assembled their vassals and fortified the Church as had been done of old against the Turks. For whenever a priest contrived by force or fraud to celebrate mass or perform any other ceremony of his religion in a church, it was considered by law to belong to him thenceforth, and to his creed. Here was a premium upon trickery and violence.

All this was in defiance of the renewed pledges entered into when Hungary yielded adhesion to Charles the Sixth's Pragmatic Sanction,* regulating the succession in his family. He wanted to transmit his kingdoms to his daughter Maria Theresa, and much diplomacy was necessary to secure the consent of States to whom a female ruler was unknown. At every Diet the Protestants made a battle for their rights, and if they apparently gained

* Pragmatic Sanction is a term that has been used in reference to various imperial or royal ordinances in history. Another equally celebrated Pragmatic Sanction was that of Charles the Seventh of France, in 1438, restricting the authority of the pope over the Gallican Church.

anything by the pressure of the moment, it was afterward undone by the bigots. This very Diet of Presburg, which recognized the baby Maria Theresa (three years old) as future queen of Hungary, was also memorable for a solemn protest from the clergy, headed by the cardinal prince of Saxony, against "any proposed toleration whatever toward those who are not Catholics." Does it not faithfully reflect the spirit of Rome in all ages?

One specimen of subsequent hardships may be given. A poor Slavack at Miawa had been much distressed in his soul on account of his sins, and finding no relief from the ceremonies and penances of the Romish Church, he went to the Protestant pastor, Daniel Kirmann. Hearing of that blessed Saviour who taketh away the sin of the world, and hath a special welcome for the weary and heavy-laden, he found peace and joy in simple believing. But as soon as the priest learned that he had joined the Protestant congregation, he brought a company of soldiers to seize and punish him. The citizens rang the alarm-bells, a mob collected; the pastor would not give up his convert, and was upheld in his resolve by the people. This scene was made the pretext for an order that they should surrender their church and school to the Catholics; the un-

Daniel Kirman.

fortunate convert was imprisoned at Presburg, and four years afterward disappeared altogether and was never more heard of. The pastor was sentenced to imprisonment for life; and though the powerful Frederick William of Prussia interceded for him, he died in jail after nine years' close confinement.

Frederick William also appealed to his imperial brother on behalf of the whole Protestant Church in Hungary. The appeal was supported by the ambassadors of England, Holland, Denmark, Sweden. But hardly anything was gained; even the oath, "by the Holy Virgin and Saints," was only suspended for a time.

CHAPTER XXXVII.

MARIA THERESA.

EVERYTHING was hoped from the kind heart of a woman when she began her reign. Nobly did Hungary stand by her in her sore distress, when Prussia, France, Spain, and Bavaria tried to overthrow her throne, established by her father on the Pragmatic Sanction. A Diet was assembled at Presburg, and one of the most striking scenes in history is that of the young queen standing in the midst of the magnates with her baby son in her arms, and addressing them in Latin so eloquently that five hundred swords flashed from their scabbards, and the cry rang to the roof, "We will die for our *king* Maria!"

Of course she would take any oath required at such a juncture; and accordingly swore "to preserve inviolate all the rights and privileges of the nation in all points, clauses and articles, as have been settled between the king and the representatives of the country." This certainly included the toleration so often granted in theory to her Protestant subjects, and so invariably broken in practice. But very soon we find the old system of petitioning begun again; for the oath above mentioned shut out Protestants from every public employment and municipal office; and they were allowed no schools nor books, and their pastors were not permitted to visit the sick and dying. They wanted an oath with the Virgin's name omitted; that those who came to worship should not be robbed or stripped; that converts should not be publicly scourged; that forcible seizure of Protestant property should be discountenanced; that complaints should not be investigated by the very parties who caused the injustice.

Maria Theresa's answer was a confirmation of her father's celebrated Resolutions, and especially of the objectionable oath "by the Virgin and saints." No act of her life shows any tenderness to that large section of her subjects who adhered to the Augsburg and Helvetic Confessions.

There was a Reformed preacher named Mathias Bohil, whose story is aptly illustrative of the times under Maria Theresa. He lived in one of the most sorely-tried evangelical cities, Eperges; that is, he was allowed to live in the suburbs, and if any sick member of his flock within the walls wanted his services, the sick man must be carried outside those walls in order to receive them. But this pastor was a dauntless person, and made himself so troublesome by maintaining his few rights that the ecclesiastics resolved to get rid of him. He had lately helped a Protestant child to escape from the hands of the Jesuits to a place where he could be educated in the faith his father wished him to learn. But because he had been forced into popery, and said he would sooner die ten deaths than have his child trained in the same, the Jesuits seized the child—six years old—and by administering the consecrated wafer made him a Catholic. Then the pastor helped the parents to send away their child; for which the father was thrown into a dungeon with a chain round his neck, while the mother (a Protestant) was forced to escape to the mountains.

Mathias Bohil could expect nothing but to be a marked man. One evening, as he was sitting at supper with his wife and children, two police-officers entered and arrested him. Before departure he contrived to secrete a line on which clothes were dried, and which afterward stood him in good service. Before the magistrates he was examined respecting a book which had appeared in Bohemian, called "The Rise and Progress of Popery," and which contained an address from the Wittemberg Church encouraging their persecuted brethren to be steadfast. His books and papers were searched, and his enemies pretended that therein were found treasonable letters to Frederick William of Prussia, the great antagonist of Maria Theresa.

When the prisoner noticed that his confinement was made more stringent and his guards doubled, watching and sleeping alternately during the twenty-four hours, he began to think that Kirmann's fate of perpetual imprisonment might be awaiting him. He resolved to attempt an escape, and having committed his case to God in prayer, "he felt such joy and inward peace as if he were already in a place of safety."

Now, it was the duty of the sentinels to relieve each other in watch, one sleeping while the other marched to and fro, but this night both seemed overcome with drowsiness. The pastor prayed that their sleep might be solid as that of Saul and Abner when David passed unobserved through the camp of his foes. Then he rose up silently and stole to the door, having with him the rope he brought from home. The key was inside, and he opened the door easily. With little trouble he reached the courtyard. The fierce dogs kept there were silent and quiet. He reached the city wall and let himself down by his rope. His hands were cut, and he had fallen some distance because the cord was short, but he was safe for the present.

Bohil lay in the woods for some days, though it was the season of melting snows. At last he was able to get across the frontier. His wife was threatened with the heaviest punishment if she dared to go after him, yet she contrived ere long to join him at Breslau with their three children. There he wrote and printed an account of the miserable state of the Evangelical Church of Hungary, in hope of attracting the sympathies of Protestant princes.

Shortly afterward a Hungarian bishop published a pamphlet dedicated to Maria Theresa, demanding the extirpation or banishment of all Protestants in the realm, and remarked in a witty manner that as the Church of Rome was never bloodthirsty, she would be quite satisfied with the burning of these heretics!

CHAPTER XXXVIII.

JOSEPH THE SECOND.

THE infant son who had been held in Maria Theresa's arms at the Diet of Presburg had since been growing into a man, and slowly strengthening with his strength was a deep-rooted hate of the priestcraft by which he saw his mother surrounded and her kingdoms imperilled. He was aware of the spirited remonstrance of Frederick of Prussia, wherein he states that "one might almost suppose the design of the government was to drive the Protestants of Hungary to despair, and induce them to try such illegal means of redress as should place them entirely at the mercy of their rulers." Often had they been driven so far in preceding generations. The marvel was that any one in Hungary had courage to be anything but a Roman Catholic, or that a vestige of the incessantly-persecuted Church survived.

Frederick's remonstrance bore fruit in an unexpected quarter. Pope Benedict the Fourteenth wrote to the cardinal of Breslau that he did not approve of the exertions of the hierarchy in Hungary. At the same time a letter from the archbishop of Canterbury stated that King George of England had given directions to his Viennese ambassador to help the Protestants in Hungary.

But the succeeding pope, Clement the Thirteenth, showed different ideas from Benedict in his fanatical Bull of 1759, wherein he calls on General Count Daun utterly to eradicate all satanic heresy. At his side would fight the destroying angel to help in annihilating the accursed seed of Luther and Calvin. Only one hundred and six years ago since the infallible head of the infallible Church used this language!

Joseph became king of Hungary shortly after. Although the jealousy of his mother left him little real power during her lifetime, yet it was now that he gathered that knowledge and formed those plans which afterward came to fruition in the great Edict of Toleration which has made his name so justly famous. He travelled throughout his kingdom and saw for himself the state of parties. He attributed much of the miseries he beheld to Jesuit interference. He proved to his mother how these Jesuits used even the secrets of the confessional for political purposes, by obtaining from Madrid a copy of the sins which she had at Easter confessed to her Jesuit priest. He rejoiced loudly when Pope Clement the Fourteenth decreed the suspension of the order.

As the empress left affairs more and more in the hands of her vigorous and clear-sighted son, the authority of the Roman Church became more limited and the liberty of the Protestants greater.

Joseph was no sooner emperor than his Protestant subjects addressed him, as usual on an accession, asking for their long-claimed rights as men and citizens. He at once ordered that religious opinions should exclude from no civil office, and that fitness should be the only qualification.

"I have a heavy work before me," he wrote to the archbishop of Salzburg; "I must reduce the army of monks and try to transform these fakirs into human beings. My task is to lessen the power of those men before whose shorn heads the rabble bows with reverence." Again, to the legate at Rome, he said, "It is necessary to remove out of the category of religion some things which never belonged to it. . . . I shall give my people, instead of a legendary romance, a preached gospel."

CHAPTER XXXIX.

THE EDICT OF TOLERATION.

IT appeared on the twenty-fourth of October, 1781—a white day in the annals of the Hungarian Church. "Perfect freedom for the Protestants"—that dream of nigh three hundred years—was at last granted and guaranteed irrevocably.

No need to examine the provisions of the edict in detail. The long and weary strife of the Evangelical Church was at last over. Gradually, by supplementary decrees, the emperor drew off any chains that remained on her shackled limbs.

Joseph the Second had need of all his strong character to stand the ensuing storm of priestly disapprobation. His confessor declared that he could promise him no success against his enemies if he did not cut off the heretics, root and branch. But the emperor only wrote to his bishops, commanding them to fulfil the law of Christ: "Whatsoever ye would that men should do to you, do ye even so to them." Any prelate who was dissatisfied with his measures of toleration could resign his office and leave the country.

The pope (Pius the Sixth) thought he would try the effect of a personal visit to his imperial son. He was received with the utmost honour. Crowds of the highest rank pressed to kiss his jewelled slipper; and his Holiness was so considerately courteous as to order the said slipper to be carried round to the house of many distinguished families in Vienna. When the pope's throne was raised a step higher than that of the emperor in the cathedral, Joseph stayed at home indisposed and cogitating new plans of religious reform. "He was no theologian; he could not argue," was his answer to every attempt at conversation on the subject. He would be glad to have the approbation of his Holiness for the Toleration Edict; but, if not convenient, it could be dispensed with! Joseph was imperturbable to smiles or frowns. When Pius went away, he accompanied him affectionately as far as the monastery of St. Mary's Well, outside the city four miles, and after he had gone quietly ordered the suppression of the monastery.

All attempts at persecution for the rest of that reign were, to use the Hungarian historian's comparison, "like isolated clouds trying to darken the bright heavens." The illustrious Joseph took care that while he lived his edict was no dead letter. "In the sweat of his brow he eat kingly bread, attempting to sweep away the arrears of ages."

Here our sketches of the Reformation in Hungary come to an end. We know that in after years there have been renewed oppressions upon the Church which battled so gallantly and so long in the cause of the truth; and also that false teachers, creeping in with false doctrines, have exposed her to the worse danger of the two. But the dawn of better days has begun. Shall we end with Luther's prayer for Hungary—an echo over three centuries applicable still?—

"O Lord God, have mercy on this poor land. Confound the devil according to thy great power. Protect thy Church against thy foes. Glorify thy Son!"

THE END.

www.ingramcontent.com/pod-product-compliance
Lightning Source LLC
LaVergne TN
LVHW011229110826
845150LV00006B/1585